The Complete works of

Rules for the Direction of the Mind

René Descartes

1628

A New Translation with introduction by
Newcomb Livraria Press

Copyright © 2023 Tim Newcomb
All rights reserved.

All rights reserved under International and Pan-American Copyright Conventions. Published in the United States. The writings of Descartes are now in the public domain in the European Union and the United States as they were printed in the early 17th century.

Original translation by Newcomb Livraria Press 2023 from the original French, Latin German 1st-edition printings using hybrid methods. Translation is as literal as possible, and multiple manuscripts were reconciled to provide the most robust translation possible.

Quotations may be used for personal and commercial purposes.

No copyright claim is made with respect to public domain works. This edition contains minor editorial revisions in the translation of the original text. Cover design by Newcomb Livraria Press utilizing Canva Pro Content License Agreement Section 5 and paid Midjourney license. The information contained in this book is provided for educational and informational purposes only and is not intended as medical or psychological advice. The author, publisher, and translators assume no responsibility or liability for any errors or omissions in the content of this book or any actions taken by the reader based on the information provided.

Contents

Introduction by the Translator **4**

Rules for the Direction of the Mind **6**

Afterword by the Translator **65**
Timeline of Descartes Life & Works **76**
Glossary of Cartesian Terminology **77**
Descartes' Major Works **79**

Introduction by the Translator

Cogito, Ergo Sum

"The effect of this man on his age and the new age cannot be imagined broadly enough," declared the greatest metaphysician of his time, Hegel. Descartes is widely considered one of the founders of modern philosophy, best known for his statement "I think, therefore I am" which established the concept of the subject as the basis of knowledge. He contributed to physics, including optics, and is regarded as one of the founders of modern mechanism. In mathematics, he developed analytic geometry. Descartes' new scientific method and theories of rationality, explained in "Rules for the Direction of the Mind" (1628) and "Discourse on the Method" (1637), rejected the Medieval scholasticism taught in universities and emphasized the importance of using method of skeptical reasoning to determine truth. His method was influenced by mathematics and aimed to replace the Aristotelian syllogistic reasoning used in the Middle Ages. As Kant said- "Descartes was the first to bring to light the idea of a transcendental science, which is to contain a system of knowledge of the conditions of possibility of all knowledge." This was the foundation of Continental Philosophy, the field of Metaphysics, the Scientific Method, and the groundwork for the Enlightenment.

Ecce Homo

Born in 1996 in La Haye en Touraine, France to a noble family, René Descartes had a Jesuit education and from his youth was an autodidact in ancient literature, philosophy, mathematics, chemistry, astronomy and physics. Galileo was still alive at the same time as Descartes, and Newton was born in his lifetime. He studied law at nearby University of Poitiers, but he quickly became disillusioned with the legal profession and turned his attention to philosophy and mathematics. The town of La Haye en Touraine is now simply renamed "Descartes".

At 18, he made his way to the big city. In Paris, he soon bored of society and moved to a suburb where he focused in isolation on Mathematics. He was enlisted into military service and was stationed in the Netherlands, and in 1619, in the first year of the Thirty Years' War, volunteered in the Bavarian troops and participated in several campaigns under Johann Tserclaes, Count of Tilly. Still, he studied relentlessly, including in Ulm where he sought after Mathematicians. Here in the winter quarters he studied diligently and made acquaintance, for example, in Ulm with a citizen who was an expert in mathematics. During winter quarters in Neuburg an der Donau, Bavaria, he first had the impulse to not merely study, but contribute, and try to build a new path for philosophy. Still a pious Catholic, he vowed to the Mother of God that he would make a pilgrimage to Loretto if she would let him succeed.

He spent much of his remaining youth traveling throughout Europe, and engaging with other intellectuals of his time. In 1621 he left the war services and made several more long journeys through the rest of Germany, then Poland, back through Prussia, Switzerland, Italy and then home to France.

Eventually, he landed in the Netherlands because of the freedom to study, and here he wrote the lion's share of his great works. Between 1629 to 1644, he wrote and published most of his writings and also defended them attacks, especially from the clergy, which he openly solicited. His famous *Meditations* was circulated to academics first and then he published it with their objections and his replies to these objections, demonstrating how intellectually honest he was and dedicated to truth. He enthusiastically welcomed criticism, writing he is "glad if people make as many objections as possible and the strongest they can find'.

Queen Christine of Sweden finally summoned him to her court in the Swedish capital, which was the gathering place of the most famous scholars of the time; and there he died in 1650. His prayer to the Theotokos in the winter cold of that small Bavarian town did not go unanswered; he became widely regarded as the founder of modern philosophy, and there is barely a culture in the world which does not use concepts of Cartesian rationality.

In the Rules for the Direction of the Mind, Descartes lays out a method for arriving at certain knowledge. He believed that traditional methods of inquiry were flawed and that a new approach was needed. The Rules propose a systematic approach to thinking that involves breaking down complex problems into simpler ones, and then working from the simplest to the most complex. This method is known as the method of analysis, and it forms the basis of Descartes' scientific method.

According to Descartes, the key to this method is to use reason to arrive at clear and distinct ideas that are free from doubt. This approach was revolutionary because it emphasized the importance of reason and rationality in arriving at knowledge. Descartes' Rules for the Direction of the Mind helped to establish the importance of rational inquiry in modern philosophy and science.

Tim Newcomb
Stuttgart, Germany
Spring 2023

Rules for the Direction of the Mind

First Rule

The purpose of study must be to direct the mind so that it makes sound and true judgments about everything that comes before it.

Whenever men perceive a resemblance between two things, they are in the habit of applying to both, even in what they differ, what they have recognized to be true of one of the two. Thus they compare, in a bad way, the sciences which consist only in the work of the mind, with the arts which need a certain use and a certain bodily disposition. And as they see that one man cannot be sufficient to learn all the arts at once, but that he alone becomes skilled in them who cultivates only one, because the same hands can hardly plow the earth and touch the lyre, and lend themselves at the same time to such diverse offices, they think that it is so with the sciences; and distinguishing them from each other by the objects they deal with, they believe that they must be studied separately and independently of each other. But this is a great mistake; for as the sciences together are nothing other than the human mind, which remains one and always the same whatever the variety of objects to which it is applied, without this variety bringing to its nature more changes than the diversity of the objects brings to the nature of the sun which illuminates them, there is no need to circumscribe the human mind within any limits; Indeed, the knowledge of a truth is not the same as the practice of an art; one truth discovered helps us to discover another, far from being an obstacle. And certainly it seems astonishing to me that most men carefully study plants and their virtues, the course of the stars, the transformations of metals, and a thousand similar objects, and that scarcely any of them concern themselves with intelligence or with this universal science of which we speak; and yet if the other studies have something to be esteemed, it is not so much for themselves as for the help they give to this one. It is not without reason that we place this rule at the head of all the others; for nothing distracts us more from the search for truth than to direct our efforts towards particular goals, instead of turning them towards this single and general end. I am not speaking here of evil and reprehensible aims, such as vain glory and the search for shameful gain; it is clear that lies and the little tricks of vulgar minds will lead to them by a shorter route than a solid knowledge of the truth could. I mean here to speak of honest and praiseworthy aims; for they are for us a subject of illusions from which we can hardly defend ourselves. Indeed, we study the useful sciences either for the advantages that we derive from them in life, or for the pleasure that we find in the contemplation of truth, and which, in this world, is almost the only pure and unmixed happiness. These are two legitimate objects that we can propose to ourselves in the study of the sciences; but if, in the midst of our work, we come to think about them, it is possible that a little haste will cause us to neglect many things that would be necessary for the knowledge of others, because at first sight they will seem to us either not very useful or not very worthy of our curiosity. What we must first recognize is that the sciences are so closely linked together that it is easier to learn them all at once than to detach one from the others. If, therefore, one wishes to search seriously for the truth, one should not apply oneself to a single science; they are all connected and mutually dependent on each other. One must think of increasing one's natural lights, not in order to be able to solve this or that difficulty of the school, but so that the intelligence can show the will the course it must take in each situation of life. He who follows this method will see that in a short time he will have made marvelous progress, and far superior to that of men who devote themselves to special studies, and that if he has not obtained the results that they want to achieve, he has reached a higher goal, and to which their wishes would never have dared to aspire.

Rule two

We must only deal with those objects of which our mind seems capable of acquiring a certain and indubitable knowledge.

All science is a certain and obvious knowledge; and he who doubts many things is no more learned than he who has never thought about them, but he is less learned than he is if he has formed false ideas about some of these things. So it is better never to study than to deal with such difficult matters that, unable to distinguish the true from the false, one is obliged to accept as certain what is doubtful; indeed, one runs more risk of losing the knowledge one has than of increasing it. This is why we reject by this rule all those knowledges which are only probable; and we think that one can only trust those which are perfectly verified, and on which one cannot raise any doubt. And although scholars may think that knowledge of this kind is very little, because, no doubt, by a natural vice of the human mind, they have neglected to pay attention to these objects, as being too easy and within the reach of all, I am not afraid to declare to them that they are more numerous than they think, and that they are sufficient to demonstrate with evidence an infinite number of propositions, on which they have so far been able to express only probable opinions, opinions which soon, thinking it unworthy of a scientist to admit that he is ignorant of something, they got used to adorning with false reasons, so that they ended up persuading themselves of them, and spouting them as proven things.

But if we strictly observe our rule, there will be few things left to study. There is scarcely a single question in the sciences on which men of mind have not differed. Now, whenever two men pass a contrary judgment on the same thing, it is certain that one of them is mistaken. Moreover, neither of them possesses the truth; for if he had a clear view of it, he could expose it to his adversary in such a way that it would eventually force his conviction. We cannot, therefore, hope to obtain complete knowledge of all those things about which we have only probable opinions, because we cannot, without presumption, expect more from ourselves than others have been able to do. It follows from this that if we count well, only geometry and arithmetic remain among the sciences, to which the observation of our rule brings us back.

We do not condemn for that the way of philosophizing to which one has stopped until now, nor the use of probable syllogisms, excellent weapons for the fights of the dialectic. Indeed, they exercise the mind of young men, and awaken in them the activity of emulation. Besides, it is better to train their minds to opinions, even uncertain ones, since they have been a subject of controversy among scholars, than to leave them to themselves, free and without guidance; for then they would run the risk of falling into precipices; but as long as they follow the traces that have been marked out for them, even though they may sometimes deviate from the true path, it is always the case that they are advancing along a safer road, at least insofar as it has been recognized by the most skilled. And we too congratulate ourselves on having been educated at school in the past; But since we are now free from the oath that bound us to the words of the teacher, and since, having reached a sufficiently mature age, we have withdrawn our hand from the blows of the schoolmaster, if we are serious about proposing rules to ourselves, by means of which we can reach the pinnacle of human knowledge, let us put the one we have just stated in the first place, and let us beware of abusing our leisure, neglecting, as many people do, easy studies, and applying ourselves only to difficult things. They may, it is true, form subtle conjectures and probable systems on these things; but, after much work, they will end by realizing that they have increased the sum of doubts, without having learned any science.

But as we have said above that, among the sciences, only arithmetic and geometry are entirely free from falsity or uncertainty, to give the exact reason, let us notice that we arrive at the knowledge of things by two ways, namely, experience and deduction. Moreover, experience is often misleading; deduction, on the other hand, or the operation by which one thing is inferred from another, may not be done, if it is not perceived, but is never done badly, even by the mind least accustomed to reasoning. This operation does not borrow much help from the bonds in which dialectic embarrasses human reason, thinking to lead it; although I am far from denying that these forms cannot serve other purposes. Thus, all the errors into which animals, but men, can fall, come, not from a false induction, but from the fact that we start from certain experiences that are not well understood, or that we make haphazard judgments that do not rest on any solid basis.

All this shows how it is that arithmetic and geometry are much more certain than the other sciences, since their object alone is so clear and simple, that they need not suppose anything that experience can revoke in doubt, and that both proceed by a chain of consequences that reason deduces from each other. They are therefore the easiest and clearest of all the sciences, and their object is as we wish it to be; for, apart from inattention, it is scarcely conceivable that a man should go astray. It is not to be wondered at, however, that many minds apply themselves in preference to other studies or to philosophy. Indeed, everyone is more confident of guessing in an obscure subject than in a clear one, and it is much easier to have a few vague ideas on any question than to arrive at the truth even on the easiest of all. From all this we must conclude, not that arithmetic and geometry are the only sciences that must be learned, but that he who seeks the path to truth must not concern himself with an object of which he cannot have a knowledge equal to the certainty of arithmetical and geometrical demonstrations.

Rule Three

It is necessary to seek on the object of our study, not what others have thought of it, nor what we suspect ourselves, but what we can see clearly and with evidence, or deduce in a certain way. This is the only way to arrive at science.

We must read the works of the ancients, because it is a great advantage to be able to make use of the works of so many men, firstly to know the good discoveries they have made, and secondly to be warned of what is still to be discovered. It is to be feared, however, that reading their works too attentively will leave in our minds some errors which take root there in spite of our precautions and our care. Usually, in fact, whenever a writer has allowed himself to be led by credulity or thoughtlessness to a contested opinion, there are no reasons, no subtleties that he does not use to bring us to his feeling. On the contrary, if he is fortunate enough to find something certain and obvious, he presents it to us only in an obscure and embarrassing way; fearing, no doubt, that the simplicity of the form would diminish the beauty of the discovery, or perhaps because he envies us the distinct knowledge of the truth.

Moreover, even if the authors were all frank and clear, and never gave us any doubt as to the truth, but stated what they knew in good faith; as there is scarcely a thing put forward by one of them that cannot be found to be the opposite of what is maintained by the other, we would always be uncertain as to which of the two to believe, and it would be of no use to us to count the votes in order to follow the opinion that has the greatest number in its favor. Indeed, if it is a matter of a difficult question, it is believable that the truth is rather on the side of the few than of the many. Even if all were to agree, it would still not be enough for us to know their doctrine; indeed, to use a comparison, we will never be mathematicians, even if we know by heart all the demonstrations of others, if we are not capable of solving any kind of problem by ourselves. In the same way, even if we had read all the reasonings of Plato and Aristotle, we would not be philosophers if we could not make a sound judgment on any question. We would indeed seem to have learned not a science, but history.

Let us be careful, moreover, never to mix any conjecture with our judgments about the truth of things.

This remark is of great importance; and if in vulgar philosophy one finds nothing so obvious and so certain that does not give rise to some controversy, perhaps the best reason is that the learned, not content with recognizing things that are clear and certain, have dared to affirm obscure and unknown things that they could only reach by means of conjecture and probability; Then, successively adding a complete belief in them themselves, and mixing them indiscriminately with true and obvious things, they were unable to conclude anything that did not seem to derive more or less from one of these uncertain propositions, and which was therefore uncertain.

But, in order not to fall into the same error, let us report here the means by which our understanding can rise to knowledge without fear of making mistakes. Now there are two such means, intuition and deduction. By intuition I mean not the variable testimony of the senses, nor the misleading judgment of the naturally disordered imagination, but the conception of an attentive mind, so distinct and clear that it has no doubt about what it understands; or, what amounts to the same thing, the obvious conception of a sound and attentive mind, a conception which is born of the sole light of reason, and is more certain because it is simpler than the deduction itself, which however, as I said above, cannot fail to be well done by man. Thus everyone can see intuitively that he exists, that he thinks, that a triangle is terminated by three lines, neither more nor less, that a globe has only one surface, and so many other things which are more numerous than is commonly thought, because we disdain to pay attention to such easy things.

But lest anyone be confused by the new use of the word intuition, and of some others that I will be obliged to use in the future in a sense that deviates from the vulgar meaning, I want to warn here in general that I am not very concerned about the meaning that the school has given to the words in recent times; It would be very difficult indeed to use the same terms to represent very different ideas; but let me only consider what meaning they have in Latin, so that, whenever I lack the proper expression, I use the metaphor that seems to me the most suitable to convey my thought.

Now this evidence and this certainty of intuition must be found not only in any utterance, but in all reasoning. Thus when we say two and two are the same as three and one, we must not only see by intuition that two and two equal four, and that three and one equal four, we must also see that from these two propositions it is necessary to conclude this third one, namely, that they are equal.

One might perhaps wonder why we add to intuition this other way of knowing by deduction, that is, by the operation which, from a thing of which we have certain knowledge, draws consequences that are necessarily deduced from it. But we have had to admit this new mode; for there are many things which, without being self-evident, nevertheless bear the character of certainty, provided they are deduced from true and undisputed principles by a continuous and uninterrupted movement of thought, with a distinct intuition of each thing; just as we know that the last ring of a long chain holds to the first, even though we cannot embrace at a glance the intermediate rings, provided that, after having gone through them successively, we remember that, from the first to the last, they all hold together. So we distinguish intuition from deduction, in that in the one we conceive a certain course or succession, whereas it is not so in the other, and furthermore that deduction does not need present evidence like intuition, but borrows all its certainty, as it were, from memory; from which it follows that we can say that the first propositions, derived immediately from the principles, can be, according to the way of considering them, known sometimes by intuition, sometimes by deduction; whereas the principles themselves are known only by intuition, and the remote consequences only by deduction.

These are the two surest ways of arriving at science; the mind must not admit any more; it must reject all others as suspect and subject to error; This does not prevent the truths of revelation from being the most certain of all our knowledge, for the faith which founds them is, as in all that is obscure, an act not of the mind, but of the will, and if it has any foundation in the human intelligence, it is by one of the two ways of which I have spoken that it can and must be found, as I shall perhaps show some day with more detail.

rule four.

Necessity of the method in the search of the truth.

Men are driven by such blind curiosity that they often direct their minds into unknown paths, without any well-founded hope, but only to try whether what they are looking for might not be there; much like one who, in the foolish ardor of discovering a treasure, would perpetually scour all the places to see if some traveler had not left one there; it is in this spirit that almost all chemists, most geometers, and a good number of philosophers study. And certainly I do not deny that they sometimes have the happiness of encountering some truth; but I do not grant that they are for that reason more skilful, but only happier. So it is better never to think of seeking the truth than to attempt it without method; for it is certain that studies without order and confused meditations obscure the natural lights and blind the mind. This is confirmed by experience, since we see men who have never been occupied with literature judge in a more sound and reliable way what is presented than those who have spent their lives in schools. Now, by method, I mean certain and easy rules, which, if followed rigorously, will prevent one from ever assuming what is false, and will ensure that without consuming one's strength uselessly, and by gradually increasing one's knowledge, the mind will rise to the exact knowledge of all that it is capable of achieving.

It is necessary to note these two points, not to suppose true what is false, and to try to arrive at the knowledge of all things. Indeed, if we are ignorant of anything we can know, it is because we have never noticed any means that could lead us to such knowledge, or because we have fallen into the opposite error. Now if the method shows clearly how we must use intuition to avoid mistaking the false for the true, and how deduction must operate to lead us to the knowledge of all things, it will be complete in my opinion, and nothing will be lacking, since there is no science except with intuition and deduction, as I have said above. However, it cannot go so far as to learn how these operations are done, because they are the simplest and the first of all; so that if our mind did not know how to do them in advance, it would not understand any of the rules of the method, however easy they might be. As for the other operations of the mind, which dialectic endeavors to direct with the help of these first two means, they are of no use here; moreover, they must be counted among the obstacles; for nothing can be added to the pure light of reason that does not obscure it in some way.

As the usefulness of this method is such that to devote oneself without it to the study of letters is rather a harmful thing than useful, I like to think that for a long time the superior minds, abandoned to their natural direction, have in some way glimpsed it. Indeed, the human soul possesses something divine in which are deposited the first seeds of useful knowledge, which, in spite of the negligence and embarrassment of poorly done studies, bear spontaneous fruit. We have a proof of this in the easiest of all sciences, arithmetic and geometry. It has indeed been noted that the ancient geometers used a kind of analysis, which they extended to the solution of problems, even though they envied posterity its knowledge. And do we not see a certain kind of arithmetic, algebra, flourishing, whose aim is to do with numbers what the ancients did with figures? Now these two analyses are nothing other than the spontaneous fruits of the principles of this natural method, and I am not surprised that, applied to such simple objects, they have succeeded more happily than in other sciences where greater obstacles have prevented their development; although even in these sciences, provided they are cultivated with care, they can reach full maturity.

This is the aim I propose in this treatise. Indeed, I would not make much use of these rules if they only served to solve certain problems which calculators and geometers amuse their leisure time. In that case, what would I do but to deal with trifles with perhaps more subtlety than others? Also, although in this treatise I often speak of figures and numbers, because there is no science from which one can borrow more obvious and certain examples, he who will follow my thought carefully will see that I am not embracing anything less than ordinary mathematics, but that I am exposing another method, of which they are rather the envelope than the substance. Indeed, it must contain the first rudiments of human reason, and help to bring out of any subject the truths it contains; and, to speak freely, I am convinced that it is superior to any other human means of knowledge, because it is the origin and source of all truths. Now I say that mathematics is the envelope of this method, not that I want to hide it and wrap it up, to keep the common man away from it; on the contrary, I want to clothe and adorn it, so that it is more within the reach of the mind.

When I began to devote myself to mathematics, I read most of the works of those who cultivated it, and I studied arithmetic and geometry in preference, because they were, it was said, the simplest, and like the key to all the other sciences; but I did not find in either of them an author who satisfied me completely. I saw various propositions on numbers, the truth of which, when calculated, I recognized; as for figures, many truths were put before my eyes, so to speak, and some others were concluded by analogy; but I did not seem to be told clearly enough why things were as they were shown, and by what means their discovery was achieved. Therefore, I was no longer surprised that skilled and learned men abandoned these sciences, after having barely touched them, as puerile and vain knowledge, or, on the other hand, trembled to engage in them, as in difficult and embarrassing studies. Indeed, there is nothing more empty than to occupy oneself with numbers and imaginary figures, as if one wanted to stop at the knowledge of such trifles; and to apply oneself to these superficial demonstrations that chance discovers more often than art, to apply oneself to them, I say, with so much care, that one disapproves, as it were, of using one's reason; not to mention that there is nothing more difficult than to free, by this method, the new difficulties which present themselves for the first time, from the confusion of numbers which envelop them. But when, on the other hand, I asked myself why the first inventors of philosophy wanted to admit to the study of wisdom only those who had studied mathematics, as if this science had been the easiest of all and the most necessary to prepare and train the mind to understand higher ones, I suspected that they recognized a certain mathematical science different from that of our age. It is not that I believe that they had a perfect knowledge of it: their insane enthusiasm and their sacrifices for the smallest discoveries, prove how much these studies were then in their infancy. Nor am I touched by the praise that historians lavish on some of their inventions; for, in spite of their simplicity, it is conceivable that an ignorant and easily astonished multitude praised them as prodigies. But I am persuaded that certain primitive germs of truths which nature has deposited in the human intelligence, and which we choke in us by dint of reading and hearing so many diverse errors, had, in this simple and naive antiquity, so much vigor and strength, that men enlightened by this light of reason which made them prefer virtue to pleasures, the honest to the useful, even if they did not know the reason for this preference, had formed true ideas of philosophy and mathematics, even though they could not yet push these sciences to perfection. Now, I believe to find some traces of these true mathematics in Pappus and Diophantes, who, without being of the highest antiquity, lived however many centuries before us. But I would willingly believe that the writers themselves have, by a guilty trick, suppressed the knowledge of it; like some craftsmen who hide their secret, they have perhaps feared that the ease and simplicity of their method, by popularizing it, would diminish its importance, and they have preferred to make themselves admired by leaving us, as a product of their art, a few sterile truths subtly deducted, than to teach us this art itself, the knowledge of which would have caused all our admiration to stop. Finally, some men of great spirit have, in this century, tried to raise this method; for it appears to be nothing other than what is called by the barbarous name of algebra, provided that it is freed enough from this multiplicity of figures and these inexplicable figures which crush it, to give it that clarity and that supreme facility which, according to us, must be found in true mathematics. These thoughts having detached me from the special study of arithmetic and geometry, to call me to the research of a mathematical science in general, I asked myself first of all what was meant precisely by this word mathematics, and why arithmetic and geometry only, and not astronomy, music, optics, mechanics and so many other sciences, were not considered to be part of it: for here it is not enough to know the etymology of the word. Indeed, since the word mathematics only means science, those I have named have as much right as geometry to be called mathematics; and yet there is no one who, provided he has entered a school, cannot immediately distinguish what is related to mathematics properly so called, from what belongs to the other sciences. Now, thinking carefully about these things, I have discovered that all the sciences which have as their aim the search for order and measure, are related to mathematics, that it does not matter whether it is in numbers, figures, stars, sounds or any other object that one seeks this measure, that thus there must be a general science which explains all that can be found on order and measure, taken independently of any application to a special matter, and that finally this science is called by a proper name, and since a long time consecrated by the use, namely mathematics, because it contains what the other sciences are said to be part of mathematics. And a proof that it far surpasses the sciences that depend on it, in facility and importance, is that first of all it embraces all the objects to which these apply, plus a great number of others; and that secondly, if it contains some difficulties, they exist in the others, which themselves have special difficulties that arise from their particular object, and which do not exist for the general science. Now, when everyone knows the name of this science, when its object is conceived, even without thinking much about it, why is it that the knowledge of the other sciences that depend on it is painfully sought, and that no one takes the trouble to study it itself? I would certainly be surprised if I did not know that everyone considers it to be very easy, and if I had not noticed, for some time, that the human mind, leaving aside what it thinks is easy, hurries on to new and higher objects. For me, who is conscious of my weakness, I have resolved to observe constantly, in the search for knowledge, such an order that, beginning always with the simplest and easiest, I never take a step forward to move on to others, that I do not believe I have nothing more to desire of the first. That is why I have cultivated up to now, as much as I could, this universal mathematical science, so that I believe that I will be able to devote myself in the future to higher sciences, without fearing that my efforts will be premature. But, before leaving it, I will try to gather and to put in order what I have collected of more worthy of note in my previous studies, so much to be able to find them again if necessary in this book, at the age where the memory fades, that to discharge my memory itself, and to carry in other studies a freer spirit.

rule five.

The whole method consists in the order and arrangement of the objects on which the mind must turn its efforts to arrive at some truths. To follow it, it is necessary to gradually reduce the embarrassed and obscure propositions to simpler ones, and then to start from the intuition of the latter to arrive, by the same degrees, at the knowledge of the others.

It is in this point alone that the perfection of the method consists, and this rule must be kept by him who wishes to enter science, as faithfully as the thread of Theseus by him who wishes to penetrate the labyrinth. But many people either do not think about what it teaches, or ignore it completely, or assume that they do not need it; and often they examine the most difficult questions with so little order, that they resemble someone who would like to reach the top of a high building in one jump, either by neglecting the steps that lead to it, or by not realizing that they exist. So do all astrologers, who, without knowing the nature of the stars, without even having carefully observed their movements, hope to be able to determine their effects. So do many people who study mechanics without knowing physics, and make new engines at random; and most philosophers, who, neglecting experience, believe that truth will come out of their brains like Minerva from Jupiter's forehead.

Now it is against this rule that they all sin; but because the order that is required here is so obscure and embarrassing that not everyone can recognize what it is, it is to be feared that by wanting to follow it one will go astray, unless one carefully observes what will be explained in the following rule.

rule six.

In order to distinguish the simplest things from those which are wrapped up, and to follow this research with order, it is necessary, in each series of objects, where from some truths we have deduced other truths, to recognize which is the simplest thing, and how all the others depart from it more or less, or equally.

Although this rule does not seem to teach anything new, it nevertheless contains the whole secret of the method, and there is none more useful in this whole treatise. It teaches us that all things can be classified into different series, not in so far as they relate to any kind of being (a division which would fall into the categories of the philosophers), but in so far as they can be known from one another, so that when we encounter a difficulty, we can recognize whether there are things that it is good to examine first, what they are, and in what order they should be examined.

Now, in order to do this properly, we must first note that things, for the purpose of our rule, which does not consider them in isolation, but compares them with each other in order to know one from the other, can be called either absolute or relative.

I call absolute everything that is the simple and indecomposable element of the thing in question, as, for example, everything that is considered independent, cause, simple, universal, one, equal, similar, right, etc.; and I say that the simplest is the easiest, and what we must use to arrive at the solution of questions.

I call relative that which is of the same nature, or at least has a side to it by which it can be attached to the absolute, and deduced from it. But this word also contains certain other things that I call relationships, such as everything that is called dependent, effect, compound, particular, multiple, unequal, dissimilar, oblique, etc. These relations are all the more distant from the absolute as they contain a greater number of relations subordinate to them, relations which our rule recommends to distinguish one from the other, and to observe, in their connection and mutual order, so that, passing through all the degrees, we can successively arrive at what is most absolute.

Now the whole art consists in always looking for what is more absolute. Indeed, some things are more absolute from one point of view than from another, and considered otherwise, they are more relative. Thus the universal is more absolute than the particular, because its nature is simpler; but at the same time it can be said to be more relative, because it needs individuals to exist. In the same way, some things are really more absolute than others, but are not the most absolute of all. If we look at individuals, the species is the absolute; if we look at the genus, it is the relative. In measurable bodies, the absolute is the extent; but in the extent, it is the length, etc. Finally, to make it clearer that we are considering things here, not in terms of their individual nature, but in terms of the series in which we order them in order to know them from one another, we have deliberately included the cause and the equal among the absolute things, even though they are relative in nature; for, in the language of philosophers, cause and effect are two correlative terms. However, if we want to find out what the effect is, we must first know the cause, and not the effect before the cause. Thus equal things correspond to each other; but to know the unequal, we must compare it to the equal.

In the second place, it should be noted that there are few simple and indispensable elements which we can see in themselves, independently of all others, I do not say only at first sight, but even by experience and with the help of the light which is within us. So I say that we must observe them carefully; for these are the ones we have called the simplest of each series. All the others can only be perceived by deducing them from these, either immediately and shortly, or after one or two conclusions, or a greater number, conclusions whose number must still be noted, in order to recognize whether they are distant by more or less degrees from the first and simplest proposition; such must be everywhere the sequence that can produce these series of questions, to which all research must be reduced in order to be able to examine it with method. But, because it is not easy to remember them all, and because it is not so much necessary to retain them from memory as to know how to recognize them by a certain penetration of the mind, it is necessary to train the intelligence to be able to find them again as soon as they need them. Now, to achieve this, I have found that the best way is to accustom ourselves to thinking carefully about the smallest things we have previously determined.

Thirdly, we should not begin our study by looking for difficult things; but, before tackling a question, we should collect at random and without choice the first truths that present themselves, and see if from these we can deduce others, and from these still others, and so on. Having done this, we must reflect carefully on the truths already found, and see carefully why we were able to discover some of them before others, and more easily, and recognize what they are. In this way, when we approach any question, we will know by which research we must first begin. For example, I see that the number 6 is the double of 3; I will look for the double of 6, that is to say 12; I will again look for the double of this one, that is to say 24, and of this one or 48; and from this I will deduce, which is not difficult, that there is the same proportion between 3 and 6 as between 6 and 12, that between 12 and 24, etc.; and that thus the numbers 3, 6, 12, 24, 48, are in continuous proportion. Although all these things are so simple that they seem almost puerile, they explain to me, when I think about them carefully, in what way all the questions relating to the proportions and relationships of things are wrapped up, and in what order we must seek their solution, which contains the whole science of pure mathematics.

First I notice that I had no more difficulty in finding the double of 6 than the double of 3, and that in the same way, in all things, having found the ratio between any two quantities, I can find a large number of others which are between them in the same ratio; that the nature of the difficulty does not change, whether one is looking for three or four, or a larger number of these propositions, because one must find each one separately, and independently of each other. I then notice that even though given the magnitudes 3 and 6, I easily find a third in continuous proportion; it is not so easy for me, given the two extremes 3 and 12, to find the mean 6. This teaches me that there is another kind of difficulty here, quite different from the first; for, if one wants to find the proportional mean, one must think at the same time of the two extremes and of the ratio between them, in order to draw a new one by division; which is quite different from what one must do, when, given two quantities, one wants to find a third one which is in continuous proportion with them. I continue, and examine whether, given the quantities 3 and 24, the two proportional averages could have been found as easily as one another. And here I encounter another kind of difficulty, more embarrassing than the previous ones; for it is not necessary to think of only one or two numbers at a time, but of three, in order to discover a fourth. We can go further, and see if, given 3 and 48, it would be even more difficult to find one of the three proportional averages 6, 12, 24; this will appear at first glance; but we can see at once that the difficulty can be divided, and thus simplified, if we first look for a single average between 3 and 48, namely 24; another between 3 and 12, namely 6; then another between 12 and 48, namely 24; and that in this way we are brought back to the second difficulty, which has already been explained. From all the foregoing I notice how one can arrive at the knowledge of the same thing by two different ways, one of which is more difficult and obscure than the other. For example, to find these four numbers in continuous proportion, 3, 6, 12, 24, if one gives the two consequents 3 and 6, or 6 and 12, 12 and 24, nothing will be easier than to find the other numbers by means of these. In this case, I say that the difficulty to be solved is examined directly. If we take two terms alternatively, 3 and 12, 6 and 24, to find the others, I say that the difficulty is examined indirectly in the first way. If we take the two extremes, 3 and 24, to find the means 6 and 12, I say that the difficulty is examined indirectly in the second way. I could pursue these remarks further, and draw from this single example many other consequences; but this is enough to show the reader what I mean, when I say that a proposition is deduced directly or indirectly, and to teach him that the easiest and most elementary things, well known, can even in other studies furnish the man who puts attention and sagacity into his researches, with a great number of discoveries.

rule seven.

In order to complete science, it is necessary that the thought goes through, with an uninterrupted and continuous movement, all the objects that belong to the goal it wants to reach, and that it then summarizes them in a methodical and sufficient enumeration.

The observance of the rule here proposed is necessary in order to place among certain things those truths which, as we have said above, do not immediately derive from principles evident by themselves. Indeed, one arrives at them by such a long series of consequences, that it is not easy to remember all the path one has taken. So we say that it is necessary to make up for the faculty of memory by a continual exercise of thought. If, for example, after various operations, I find what the relationship is between the quantities A and B, then between B and C, then between C and D, finally between D and E, I do not see the relationship of the quantities A and E, and I cannot conclude it with precision from the known relationships, if my memory does not represent them all. So I will go through the sequence in such a way that the imagination sees one and moves on to another, until I can go from the first to the last with such speed that, almost without the help of memory, I can grasp the whole at a glance. This method, while relieving the memory, corrects the slowness of the mind and gives it scope.

I would add that the progress of the mind must not be interrupted; often, indeed, those who seek to draw from distant principles conclusions too quickly, cannot follow with so much care the chain of intermediate deductions that they do not miss one of them. And yet, as soon as a consequence, even the least important of all, has been forgotten, the chain is broken, and the certainty of the conclusion shaken.

I also say that science needs enumeration to be complete. Indeed, the other precepts serve to solve an infinite number of problems; but enumeration alone can make us capable of making a sure and well-founded judgment on any object to which we apply ourselves, consequently of letting absolutely nothing escape, and of having on all things certain lights.

Now here enumeration, or induction, is the careful and exact search for everything that relates to the proposed question. But this search must be such that we can conclude with certainty that we have not wrongly omitted anything. When we have used it, if the question is not clarified, at least we will be more knowledgeable, in that we will know that we cannot arrive at the solution by any of the ways known to us; and if, by chance, which happens often enough, we have been able to travel all the roads open to man to arrive at the truth, we will be able to affirm with confidence that the solution is beyond the reach of human intelligence.

It should be noted, moreover, that by sufficient enumeration or induction, we mean that means which leads us to the truth more surely than any other, except pure and simple intuition. Indeed, if the thing is such that we cannot reduce it to intuition, it is not in syllogistic forms, but in induction alone that we must put our trust. For whenever we have deduced propositions immediately from each other, if the deduction has been obvious, they will be brought back to true intuition. But if we deduce a proposition from other numerous, disjoint and multiple propositions, often the capacity of our intelligence is not such that it can embrace the whole of it in a single view: in this case the certainty of induction must suffice. Thus, without being able to distinguish with a single view all the rings of a long chain, if we have nevertheless seen the linking of these rings to each other, this will enable us to say how the first is joined to the last.

I have said that this operation must be sufficient, because it can often be defective, and thus subject to error. Sometimes, in fact, while going through a series of propositions of the greatest evidence, if we forget a single one, even the least important one, the chain is broken, our conclusion loses all its certainty. At other times we forget nothing in our enumeration, but we do not distinguish one proposition from another, and we have only a confused knowledge of the whole.

Now sometimes this enumeration must be complete, at other times distinct, sometimes it must have neither of these two characters, so I have said that it must be sufficient. Indeed, if I want to prove by enumeration how many corporeal beings there are, or which fall under the senses, I will not say that there is such a number, nor more or less, before I know with certainty that I have reported them all and distinguished them from each other. But if I want, by the same means, to prove that the rational soul is not corporeal, it will not be necessary for the enumeration to be complete; but it will suffice for me to group all bodies under a few classes, in order to prove that the soul cannot be related to any of them. If, finally, I want to show by enumeration that the area of a circle is greater than the area of all the figures whose perimeter is equal, I shall not go through all the figures, but I shall be satisfied with proving what I am saying about a few figures, and concluding it by induction for all the others.

I added that the enumeration should be methodical, because there is no better way to avoid the defects of which we have spoken, than to put order into our research, and because it often happens that if it were necessary to find separately each of the things that have to do with the principal object of our study, the whole life of a man would not suffice, either because of the number of objects, or because of the frequent repetitions that bring the same objects back under our eyes. But if we arrange all things in the best order, we shall more often than not see the formation of fixed and definite classes, of which it will suffice to know one, or to know this one rather than that other, or only something of one of them; and at least we shall not have to retrace our steps unnecessarily. This is such a good way to go, that we can easily and in a short time get to the end of a science which at first sight seemed immense.

But the order to be followed in the enumeration may sometimes vary, and depend on the whim of each person; so, in order that it may be as satisfactory as possible, it is necessary to remember what we have said in the fifth rule. In the smallest things, the whole secret of the method often consists in the happy choice of this order. Thus, do you want to make a perfect anagram by transposing the letters of a word? It will not be necessary for you to go from the easiest to the least easy, to distinguish between the absolute and the relative; these principles are not applicable here: it will be enough to draw up, in the examination of the transpositions that the letters can undergo, an order such that one never returns to the same one, then to arrange them in classes, so as to be able to recognize immediately in which one has the most hope of finding what one is seeking. Once these preparations have been made, the work will no longer be long, it will only be childish.

Moreover, our last three propositions must not be separated, but they must all be kept in mind together, because they contribute equally to the perfection of the method. It does not matter which one we put first; and if we do not develop them further here, it is because in all the rest of this treatise we will have little else to do than to explain them, by showing the particular application of the general principles we have just set out.

rule eight.

If in the series of questions there is one that our mind cannot understand perfectly, we must stop here, not examine what follows, but spare ourselves unnecessary work.

The three preceding rules trace the order and explain it; this one shows when it is necessary, when only it is useful. For what constitutes a whole degree in the scale that leads from the relative to the absolute, and vice versa, must be examined before passing beyond it; there is necessity there. But if, as often happens, many things relate to the same degree, it is always useful to go through them in order. However, the observance of the principle is not so rigorous here, and often, without knowing all these things thoroughly, only a few, or even one of them, one will be able to pass over them.

This rule necessarily follows from reasons that support the second. However, it should not be thought that it contains nothing new for the advancement of science, even though it only seems to divert us from the study of certain things, nor that it does not expose any truths, because it seems to teach students only not to waste their time, for much the same reason as the second. But those who know the seven preceding rules perfectly can learn from this one how in every science it is possible to arrive at the point of having nothing more to desire. He who, in solving a difficulty, has followed the first rules exactly, and is warned by this one to stop somewhere, will know that there is no way for him to arrive at what he is looking for, and this is not because of the fault of his mind, but because of the nature of the difficulty or of the human condition. Now, this knowledge is not a lesser science than that which enlightens us on the very nature of things, and certainly it would not be a proof of a good spirit to push one's curiosity further.

Let us clarify all this by one or two examples. If a man who knows only mathematics looks for the line called in anaclastic dioptrics, in which the parallel rays refract each other, so that after refraction they all intersect at one point, he will easily see, according to the fifth and sixth rules, that the determination of this line depends on the ratio of the angles of refraction to the angles of incidence. But since he will not be able to do this research, which is not the province of mathematics, but of physics, he will have to stop here, where it would be useless to ask the solution of this difficulty to the philosophers and to experience. He would be sinning against the third rule. Moreover, the proposition is compound and relative; and it is only in simple and absolute things that we can rely on experience, which we shall demonstrate in his place. In vain will he suppose between these various angles a relation which he will suspect to be the true one; it will not be there to seek the anaclastic, but only a line which can account for his supposition.

But if a man knowing something other than mathematics, desirous of knowing, according to the first rule, the truth about everything that presents itself to him, comes across the same difficulty, he will go further, and find that the ratio between the angles of incidence and the angles of refraction depends on their change, because of the variety of the media; that this change in turn depends on the medium, because the ray penetrates the whole of the diaphanous body; he will see that this property of penetrating a body in this way presupposes that the nature of light is known; that finally, in order to know the nature of light, it is necessary to know what a natural power is in general, which is the last and most absolute term of this whole series of questions. After having seen all these propositions clearly by means of intuition, he will go through the same stages again according to the fifth rule; and if in the second stage he cannot know the nature of light at once, he will enumerate, by the seventh rule, all the other natural powers, so that, from the knowledge of one of them, he can at least deduce by analogy the knowledge of what he does not know. Once this is done, he will seek how the ray crosses a diaphanous whole, and thus continuing the sequence of propositions, he will finally arrive at the anaclastic itself, which many philosophers, it is true, have hitherto sought in vain, but which, according to us, should offer no difficulty to the one who will know how to use our method.

But let us give the most noble example of all. Let a man set himself the task of examining all the truths which the human mind can know, a task which, in my opinion, should be undertaken at least once in their lifetime by those who seriously wish to attain wisdom. He will find, with the help of the rules I have given, that the first thing to be known is intelligence, since it is from this that the knowledge of all other things depends, and not vice versa. Then, examining what immediately follows the knowledge of pure intelligence, he will review all the other means of knowledge that we possess, not including intelligence; he will find that there are only two, imagination and the senses. He will therefore give all his care to examining and distinguishing these three means of cognition, and seeing that, strictly speaking, truth and error can only be found in the intelligence alone, and that the other two modes of cognition are only occasions for it, he will carefully avoid everything that can lead him astray, and will count all the ways that are open to man to arrive at the truth, in order to follow the right one. But they are not so numerous that he cannot easily find them all after sufficient enumeration. And what will seem astonishing and incredible to those who have not experienced it, as soon as he has distinguished the knowledge that fills or adorns the memory from that which makes the true scholar, a distinction that he will easily make.....[1] He will see that if he is ignorant of something, it is neither for lack of mind nor for lack of ability, and that there is not a thing of which another possesses the knowledge that he is not capable of knowing as he does, provided he applies his attention to it properly. And although he may often be presented with questions which our rule forbids him to investigate, since he will see that they are beyond the reach of the human mind, he will not think himself more ignorant than another; but the little he knows, that is to say, that no one can know anything about the matter, should, if he is wise, fully satisfy his curiosity.

Now, in order not to remain in a continual uncertainty about what our mind can do, and not to consume ourselves in fruitless and unhappy efforts, before approaching the knowledge of each thing in particular, we must once in our life ask ourselves what are the knowledge that human reason can attain. To succeed in this, between two equally easy means, one must always begin with the one that is more useful.

This method imitates those of the mechanical professions, which do not need the help of others, but which themselves provide the means of constructing the instruments they need. If a man, for example, wanted to practice the trade of blacksmith, and was deprived of all the necessary tools, he would be forced to use a hard stone or a coarse mass of iron; instead of an anvil, he would take a rock for a hammer, arrange two pieces of wood in the form of tongs, and thus make the instruments that are indispensable to him. When this is done, he will not begin by forging, for the use of others, swords and helmets, or anything else that is made with iron; first of all he will forge for himself hammers, an anvil, tongs, and everything else he needs. In the same way, it is not at our beginning, with a few little clarified rules, which are given to us by the very constitution of our mind earlier than they are taught to us by art, that we will have to try to reconcile the quarrels of the philosophers, and to solve the problems of the mathematicians. We will first have to use these rules to find out what is most necessary for us to examine the truth, since there is no reason why this should be more difficult to discover than any of the questions that are agitated in geometry, physics, or in the other sciences.

Now, here there is no more important question to be resolved than that of knowing what human knowledge is, and how far it extends, two things that we bring together in one and the same question that must be treated above all according to the rules given above. This is a question that must be examined once in a lifetime, when one loves truth to any extent, because this research contains all the method, and like the true instruments of science. Nothing seems to me more absurd than to discuss boldly the mysteries of nature, the influence of the stars, the secrets of the future, without having once examined whether the human mind can reach this point. And it should not seem difficult and painful to us to set the limits of our mind in this way, when we do not hesitate to pass judgment on things that are outside of us, and completely foreign to us. Nor is it an immense task to try to embrace by thought the objects which this world contains, in order to recognize how each of them can be grasped by our mind. Indeed, there is nothing so multiple and so scattered that cannot be contained within certain limits, and brought under a certain number of heads, by means of the enumeration we have spoken of. In order to experience this, in the question posed above, we shall divide into two parts everything that relates to it: it relates, in fact, either to us, who are capable of knowing; or to things, which can be known: these two points will be treated separately.

And first of all we shall notice that in us the intelligence alone is capable of knowing, but that it can be either prevented or helped by three other faculties, namely, imagination, the senses, and memory. We must therefore see successively in what way these faculties can harm us to avoid it, or help us to profit from it. This first point will be completely dealt with by a sufficient enumeration, as the following rule will show.

We must then move on to the objects themselves, and consider them only in so far as our intelligence can reach them. In this respect, we divide them into simple and complex or compound things. The simple can only be spiritual or corporeal, or spiritual and corporeal at the same time. The compound things are of two kinds: the mind finds some of them before it can say anything positive about them; it makes the others itself, an operation which will be explained at greater length in the gentle rule, where it will be shown that error can be found only in the things which the mind has composed. We shall therefore distinguish even these latter things into two kinds, those which are deduced from the simplest things, which are known by themselves; we shall devote the next book to them: and those which presuppose others, which experience teaches us are essentially composed; the third book will be entirely devoted to them.

Now in all this treatise we shall try to follow with exactitude and to smooth out the paths that can lead man to the discovery of the truth, so that the most mediocre mind, provided it is deeply penetrated by this method, will see that the truth is no more forbidden to it than to any other, and that, if it is ignorant of something, it is not for want of either mind or ability. But whenever he wants to know something, he will either find it all at once, or he will see that his knowledge depends on an experience that is not in his power to make; and then he will not blame his mind for being forced to stop at once, or he will recognize that the thing sought surpasses the efforts of the human mind; thus he will not think himself more ignorant, because to have arrived at this result is already a science worth another.

rule nine.

One must direct all the forces of one's mind to the easiest and least important things, and dwell on them for a long time, until one is accustomed to seeing the truth clearly and distinctly.

Having set forth the two operations of the intelligence, intuition and deduction, the only ones that can lead us to connoissance, we go on to explain, in this rule and in the next, by what means we may become more skillful in producing these acts, and at the same time in cultivating the two principal faculties of our mind, namely insight, by distinctly considering each thing, and sagacity, by skillfully deducing things from each other.

The way we use our eyes is enough to teach us the use of intuition. He who wishes to see many things with a single glance sees nothing distinctly; likewise he who, by a single act of thought, wishes to reach several objects at once has a confused mind. On the contrary, workers who are engaged in delicate work, and who are accustomed to direct their gaze attentively on each particular point, acquire, by practice, the facility of seeing the smallest and finest things. In the same way, those who do not divide their thoughts among a thousand different objects, but who occupy them entirely in considering the simplest and easiest things, acquire great insight.

It is a common vice among men that the most difficult things seem to them the most beautiful. Most people do not believe they know anything when they find a clear and simple cause for things; so they admire certain subtle and profound reasons of the philosophers, even though they often rest on foundations that no one has rigorously verified. This is preferring darkness to light. But it should be noted that those who really know recognize the truth with equal ease, whether they have found it in a simple or obscure subject. Indeed, it is by an act that is always distinct and always similar that they understand each truth once they have reached it; the whole difference is in the road, which must certainly be longer, if it leads to a truth that is further from the primitive and absolute principles.

It is therefore necessary to accustom oneself to embracing by thought so few objects at once, and objects so simple, that one believes oneself to know only that of which one has an intuition as clear as of the clearest thing in the world. This is a talent that has been given by nature to some much more than to others; but art and exercise can still considerably increase natural dispositions. There is only one point on which I cannot insist too much, and that is that everyone should be firmly convinced that it is not from great and difficult things, but only from the simplest and easiest things that one must deduce even the most hidden sciences.

For example, if I wanted to know if any natural power could arrive at a distant place in the same instant and pass through the medium that separates it, I would not think of the magnetic force, or the influence of the stars, or even the speed of light, in order to find out if these movements are instantaneous. This would be more difficult to prove than what I am looking for. I will rather reflect on the local movement of bodies, for there is nothing in this kind that is more sensitive, and I will notice that a stone cannot in an instant pass from one place to another, because it is a body, whereas a power similar to that which moves this stone can only be communicated instantaneously, if it passes by itself from one subject to another. Thus, when I move the end of a stick, however long it may be, I can easily conceive that the power which moves it also sets in motion in one and the same instant its other parts, because it communicates itself alone, and does not enter into a body, into a stone, for example, which carries it with it.

In the same way, if I want to recognize how one and the same cause can produce opposite effects at the same time, I will not borrow from doctors remedies that drive out certain humors and retain others; I will not say foolishly of the moon that it heats up by its heat, and cools down by its occult quality. I will look at a balance, where the same weight in one and the same moment raises one of the basins and lowers the other.

rule ten.

In order for the mind to acquire facility, it must be trained to find things that others have already discovered, and to go through with method even the most common arts, especially those that explain order or assume it.

I confess that I was born with such a mind, that the greatest happiness of study consists for me, not in hearing the reasons of others, but in finding them myself. This disposition alone excited me when I was still young to the study of the sciences; so, whenever any book promised me by its title a new discovery, before reading it any further, I tried to see if my natural sagacity could lead me to something similar, and I took great care that a hasty reading did not take away this innocent pleasure. This succeeded so many times that I finally realized that I had arrived at the truth, not like other men after blind and uncertain research, by a stroke of luck rather than by art, but that long experience had taught me fixed rules, which helped me wonderfully, and which I used in the following years to find many truths. So I practiced this method with care, convinced that from the beginning I had followed the most useful direction.

But as not all minds are equally capable of discovering the truth on their own, this rule teaches us that we must not suddenly occupy ourselves with difficult and arduous things, but begin with the least important and simplest arts, those especially where order reigns, as are the trades of the weaver, the upholsterer, the women who embroider or make lace ; as are the combinations of numbers, and all that has to do with arithmetic, so many other similar arts in a word, which wonderfully exercise the mind, provided that we do not borrow the knowledge from others, but that we discover them ourselves. Indeed, as they have nothing obscure about them, and as they are perfectly within the reach of human intelligence, they show us distinctly innumerable systems, diverse among themselves, and nevertheless regular. Now it is in rigorously observing their sequence that almost all human sagacity consists. We have also warned that we must examine these things with method; and method, in these subordinate arts, is nothing other than the constant observation of the order that is found in the thing itself, or that has been put there by a happy invention. In the same way, when we want to read unknown characters in the midst of which we discover no order, we first imagine one, either to verify the conjectures that present themselves to us about each sign, each word or each sentence, or to arrange them in such a way that we can know by enumeration what can be deduced from them. We must be especially careful not to waste our time guessing at such things by chance or without method. Indeed, although it is often possible to discover them without the help of art, and even with happiness more quickly than by method, they dull the mind, and accustom it so much to vain and puerile things, that it runs the risk of stopping at the surface without ever penetrating further. Let us beware, however, of falling into the error of those who occupy their thoughts only with serious and elevated things, of which, after much effort, they acquire only confused notions, while wanting profound ones. It is therefore necessary to begin with easy things, but with method, in order to accustom ourselves to penetrate by the open and known ways, as if by playing, to the intimate truth of things. By this means we shall become imperceptibly, and in less time than we could hope, capable of deducing with equal ease from obvious principles a great number of propositions which seem to us very difficult and very embarrassing.

Many people will perhaps be surprised that, in dealing here with the means of making ourselves more capable of deducing truths from one another, we omit to speak of the precepts of the dialecticians, who believe they direct human reason by prescribing to it certain formulas of reasoning that are so conclusive that the reason that trusts in them, even though it dispenses with giving the deduction itself careful attention, can nevertheless, by the virtue of the form alone, arrive at a certain conclusion. We notice indeed that truth often escapes from these bonds, and that those who use them remain wrapped up in them. This is what does not happen so often to those who do not make use of them, and our experience has shown us that the most subtle sophisms only deceive sophists, and almost never those who use their reason alone. Therefore, lest reason abandon us when we seek the truth in something, we reject all such formulas as contrary to our purpose, and we only gather all the help that can hold our attentive thought, as we shall show later. Now, to be more completely convinced that this syllogistic art doesn't help us discover the truth, we must notice that dialecticians can't form any syllogism which concludes the truth, without having had the matter beforehand, that is, without having known in advance the truth which this syllogism develops. From this it follows that this form gives them nothing new; that thus vulgar dialectic is completely useless to the one who wants to discover the truth, but that it can only serve to expose more easily to others the truths already known, and that thus it must be sent back from philosophy to rhetoric.

rule eleven.

After having glimpsed by intuition some simple propositions, if we conclude some other, it is useful to follow them without interrupting for a single instant the movement of thought, to reflect on their mutual relations, and to conceive distinctly at once the greatest number possible; this is the way to give our science more certainty and our mind more scope.

This is the place to explain more clearly what we said about intuition in the third and seventh rules. In the first we contrasted it with deduction, in the second only with enumeration, which we defined as a collection of several distinct things, whereas the simple operation of deducing one thing from another is done by intuition.

It must have been so; for we require two conditions for intuition, namely that the proposition appear clear and distinct, and then that it be understood all at once and not successively. Deduction, on the other hand, if, as in the third rule, we examine its formation, does not seem to take place instantaneously, but implies a certain movement of our mind inferring one thing from another; so in this rule we have rightly distinguished it from intuition. But if we consider it as done, according to what we said in the seventh rule, then it no longer designates a movement, but the term of a movement. So we suppose that it is seen by intuition when it is simple and clear, but not when it is multiple and wrapped up. Then we have given it the name of enumeration and induction, because it cannot be understood all at once by the mind, but its certainty depends in some way on memory, which must preserve the judgments made about each of the parts, in order to conclude a single judgment.

All these distinctions were necessary for the understanding of this rule. The ninth having dealt with intuition and the tenth with enuneration, the present rule explains how these two rules help and perfect each other, to the point of appearing to be one, by virtue of a movement of thought which carefully considers each object in particular and at the same time passes to other objects.

We find in this the double advantage, on the one hand of knowing with more certainty the conclusion that occupies us, and on the other hand of making our mind more apt to discover others. Indeed, memory, on which we have said that the certainty of conclusions too complex for intuition to embrace at once depends, memory, weak and fleeting by nature, needs to be renewed and strengthened by this continuous and repeated movement of thought. Thus, when, after several operations, I come to know what is the relation between a first and a second magnitude, between a second and a third, between a third and a fourth, and finally between a fourth and a fifth, I do not see the relation of the first to the fifth, and I cannot deduce it from the relations already known without remembering them all. It is therefore necessary that my thought goes through them again, until finally I can pass from the first to the last quickly enough to seem, almost without the help of memory, to embrace the totality of them in one and the same intuition.

This method, as everyone can see, remedies the slowness of the mind, and even increases its scope. But what we must also notice is that the usefulness of this rule consists especially in the fact that, accustomed to thinking about the mutual dependence of simple propositions, we acquire the habit of distinguishing at once those which are more or less relative, and by which degrees we must pass to bring them back to the absolute. For example, if I go through a number of quantities in continuous proportion, I will notice all this: Namely, that it is by an equal conception, and neither more nor less easy, that I recognize the relation of the first to the second, of the second to the third, of the third to the fourth, and so on, while it is not so easy for me to recognize in what dependence the second is on the first and the third all at once, much more difficult to recognize in what dependence the second is on the first and the fourth, and so on of the others. Hence I understand why, if I am given only the first and the second, I can find the third and the fourth and the others, because this is done by particular and distinct conceptions; if, on the other hand, I am given only the first or the third, I will not so easily discover the middle one, because this can only be done by a conception that embraces two of the preceding ones at once. If I am given only the first and the fourth, it will be even more difficult for me to find the two middle ones, because it is necessary to embrace three conceptions at once; so that consequently it would seem even more difficult, the first and the fifth being given, to find the three middle ones. But there is another reason why it should be otherwise, and that is that even though in our last example there are four conceptions joined together, it is still possible to separate them, because the number four is divided by another number. Thus I can look for the third magnitude only between the first and the fifth; then the second between the first and the third, etc. The man accustomed to thinking about this procedure, each time he examines a new question, will immediately recognize the cause of the difficulty and at the same time the simplest mode of solution of all, which is the most powerful help for the knowledge of truth.

rule twelve.

Finally, one must make use of all the resources of the intelligence, the imagination, the senses, and the memory, in order to have a distinct intuition of simple propositions, in order to compare properly what one is looking for with what one knows, and in order to find the things that must be compared among themselves; in a word, one must not neglect any of the means with which man is equipped.

This rule contains all that has been said above, and shows in general what should be explained in particular.

To arrive at knowledge, there are only two things to consider, we who know, and the objects that must be known. There are four faculties in us which we can use to know, intelligence, imagination, the senses and memory. Intelligence alone is capable of conceiving the truth. It must, however, be assisted by imagination, the senses and memory, so as not to leave any of our means unused. As for the objects themselves, there are only three things to be considered; first, we must see what offers itself to us spontaneously, then how one thing is known by another; finally, what things are deduced from others, and from which they are deduced. This enumeration seems to me to be complete; it embraces all that man's faculties can reach.

Stopping, therefore, at the first point, I would like to be able to show here what the soul of man is, what his body is, how the one is formed by the other; what are, in this complex whole, the faculties which serve for knowledge, and in what way each of them contributes to it; but the limits of this writing cannot contain all the necessary preliminaries so that these truths may be evident to all. Indeed, I always wish to write in such a way as not to pronounce anything affirmative on controversial questions, before I have set out the reasons which have led me to my opinion, and by which I think that others may also be persuaded; but as this is not permitted here, I shall suffice to indicate as briefly as possible the manner, in my opinion, most useful to my purpose, of conceiving of all the faculties which are in us destined for the acquisition of knowledge. You are free not to believe that things are like this; but who can prevent you from adopting the same suppositions, if it is evident that, without altering the truth, they only make everything clearer? just as in geometry you make suppositions about a quantity which in no way undermine the force of the demonstrations, even though physics often gives us a different idea of the nature of that quantity.

It is necessary to conceive, first of all, that the external senses, in so far as they are part of the body, although we apply them to objects by our action, that is to say, by virtue of a local movement, nevertheless feel only passively, that is to say, in the same way as wax receives the imprint of a seal. And we must not believe that this comparison is taken only from analogy, but we must conceive that the external form of the sensing body is really modified by the object, in the same way that the surface of the wax is modified by the stamp. This does not only happen when we touch a body as figurative, hard, rough, etc., but even when by tact we have the perception of heat and cold. The same is true of the other senses. Thus the initially opaque part which is in the eye receives the figure which the impression of the light tinted with different colors brings to it. The skin of the ears, the nostrils, the tongue, at first impenetrable to the object, also borrows a new figure of the sound, the smell and the savor.

It is convenient to conceive all these things in this way; indeed, nothing falls more easily under the senses than a figure: we touch it, we see it; this supposition entails no more inconvenience than any other. The proof is that the conception of the figure is so simple and so common that it is contained in every sensible object. For example, suppose that color is anything you like, you cannot deny that it is always something extended, and therefore figurative. What is the disadvantage, then, if instead of admitting a useless hypothesis, and without denying what others may think of color, we consider it only as figurative, and conceive the difference between white, blue, and red, etc., as the difference between these and other similar figures?

111

Now the same can be said of all things, since the infinite multitude of figures is sufficient to express the differences of sensible objects.

In the second place, it is necessary to conceive that at the instant when the external sense is set in motion by the object, the figure which it receives is carried to another part of the body which is called the common sense; and this instantaneously, and without there being any real passage of any being from one point to another; Just as when I write, I know that at the moment each character is drawn on the paper, not only is the lower part of my pen in motion, but also that it cannot receive the least movement that is not communicated simultaneously to the whole pen, whose upper part describes in the air the same figures, even though nothing real passes from one end to the other. Now, who could believe that the connection of the parts of the human body is less complete than that of the feather, and where could a simpler image be found to represent it?

In the third place, it is necessary to conceive that the common sense plays the role of a seal, which imprints in the imagination, as in wax, those figures or ideas which the external senses send pure and incorporeal; that this imagination is a true part of the body, and of such a size that its various parts can take on several figures distinct from one another, and even keep their imprint for a long time: in this case, it is called memory.

In the fourth place, it must be conceived that the motive power or the nerves themselves originate in the brain, which contains the imagination, which moves them in a thousand ways, as the common sense is moved by the external sense, or the whole feather by its lower extremity; An example which shows how the imagination can be the cause of a great number of movements in the nerves, without it being necessary that it should possess in itself the imprint of it, provided it possesses other imprints of which these movements may be the sequel; indeed the whole feather is not moved like its lower end. Moreover, it seems, in its greater part, to follow a quite opposite inverse movement. This explains how all the movements of all animals come about, even though they have no knowledge of things, but only a purely corporeal imagination, and how all the operations that do not need the assistance of reason are produced in us.

Fifthly and finally, we must conceive that this force by which we properly know objects is purely spiritual, and is no less distinct from the whole body than is the blood from the bones and the hand from the eye; that it is one and the same, whether it receives with the imagination the figures sent to it by the common sense, or whether it applies itself to those which the memory keeps in deposit, or whether it forms new ones, which take hold of the imagination to such an extent that it cannot suffice to receive at the same time the ideas brought to it by the common sense, or to transmit them to the motive force, according to the mode of dispensation which suits it. In all these cases, the cognizing force is sometimes passive and sometimes active; it imitates sometimes the seal, sometimes the wax; a comparison which must be taken, however, as a simple analogy; for, among material objects, there is nothing that resembles it. It is always one and the same force which, when applied with the imagination to the common sense, is called seeing, touching, etc.; to the imagination, in so far as it assumes various forms, is called remembering; to the imagination which creates new forms, is called imagining or conceiving; which finally, when it acts alone, is called understanding, which we shall explain at greater length in its place. Also it receives, because of these various faculties, the diverse names of pure intelligence, of imagination, of memory, of sensibility. It is properly called mind when it forms new ideas in the imagination, or when it applies to those already formed, and we consider it as the cause of these different operations. The distinction of these names will have to be observed later on. Once all these things are well conceived, the attentive reader will have no difficulty in concluding what help each of these faculties can be to us, and to what extent art can make up for the natural defects of the mind.

For as the intelligence can be moved by the imagination, and act upon it, as the latter in its turn can act upon the senses with the help of the motive force by applying them to objects, and as the senses on the other hand act upon it by painting there the images of bodies, as moreover the memory, at least that which is corporeal and which resembles that of the beasts, is identical with the imagination, it follows from there that if the intelligence deals with things which have nothing corporeal or analogous to the body, in vain will it hope for the help of these faculties. Moreover, in order that its action should not be stopped, it is necessary to put aside the senses, and to deprive, as far as possible, the imagination of any distinct impression. If, on the other hand, the intellect proposes to examine something that can be related to a body, it will be necessary to form in the imagination the most distinct idea possible. To achieve this more easily, it is necessary to show the external senses the very object that this idea will represent. The plurality of objects will not facilitate the distinct intuition of an individual object; but if one wishes to distract an individual from this plurality, which is often necessary, it is necessary to rid the imagination of all that could divide the attention, so that the rest is better engraved in the memory. In the same way, one should not present the objects themselves to the external senses, but only offer abbreviated images of them, which, provided they do not mislead us, will be all the better for being shorter. These are the precepts that must be observed, if we wish to omit nothing that relates to the first part of our rule.

Let us come to the second, and carefully distinguish the notions of simple things from those of compound things; let us see in which of these there may be falsity, in order to take our precautions with respect to the latter; those in which there may be certainty, in order to apply ourselves exclusively to their study. Here, as in our previous research, we must admit certain propositions which perhaps will not meet with the assent of everyone; but it does not matter if we do not believe them to be more true than those imaginary circles which serve astronomers to enclose their phenomena, provided that they help us to distinguish of which objects we can have a true or false knowledge.

We therefore say first of all that things must be considered from another point of view when we examine them in relation to our intelligence, which only knows them when we speak of them in relation to their real existence. Thus be a body extended and figured: in itself we admit that it is something one and simple; indeed, it cannot be said to be composed because it has corporality, extent, and figure, for these elements have never existed independent of each other. But, with respect to our intelligence, it is a compound of these three elements, because each of them presents itself separately to our mind, before we have time to recognize that they are all three united in one and the same subject. Thus, dealing here with things only in their relation to our intelligence, we shall call simple those only whose notion is so clear and distinct that the mind cannot divide it into other still simpler notions; such are figure, extent, motion, etc. We conceive all others as being simple, but we do not call them simple. We conceive all the others as being, as it were, composed of these; which must be understood in the most general way, without excepting even those things which it is possible for us to abstract from these simple notions, as when we say that the figure is the limit of extent, thus understanding by limit something more general than the figure, because we can say the limit of duration, of motion, etc. In this case, although the notion of limit is abstracted from that of figure, it should not appear simpler than the latter. On the contrary, since it is attributed to other things essentially different from the figure, such as duration and motion, it had to be abstracted from these notions, and consequently it is a compound of quite diverse elements, to each of which it applies only by equivocation.

We say, secondly, that the things called simple in relation to our intelligence are either purely intellectual, or purely material, or intellectual and material at the same time. Those things are purely intellectual which the intellect knows by means of a certain natural light, and without the aid of any corporeal image. Now there are many of this kind; and, for example, it is impossible to form a material image of doubt, of ignorance, of the action of the will, which I may call volition, and of so many other things, which, however, we do know, and so easily that it is sufficient for us to be endowed with reason. Those things which we know only in bodies, such as figure, extent, motion, etc., are purely material. Finally, we must call common those things that are attributed indiscriminately to bodies and spirits, such as existence, unity, duration, and the like. To this class must be related those common notions, which are like links that unite between them various simple natures, and on the evidence of which rest the conclusions of reasoning; for example, the proposition, two things equal to a third are equal to each other; and again, two things that cannot be related in the same way to a third, have some diversity between them. Now these ideas can be known, either by the pure intelligence, or by the intelligence examining the images of material objects.

Among the simple things, we must also place their negation and deprivation, insofar as they fall under our intelligence, because the idea of nothingness, of the instant, of rest, is no less true an idea than that of existence, of duration, of motion. This way of looking at things will enable us to say, in the following, that all the other things we know are composed of these simple elements; thus when I judge that a figure is not in motion, I can say that my idea is composed, in some way, of the figure and of rest, and so of the others.

Thirdly, we shall say that these simple elements are all known by themselves, and contain nothing false, which will be easily seen if we distinguish the faculty of intelligence which sees and knows things, from that which judges by affirming and denying. For it may be that we believe we are ignorant of things we really know; for example, if we suppose that besides what we see, and what we reach by thought, they still contain something unknown to us, and that this supposition is false. In this respect, it is evident that we are mistaken if we believe that we do not know any of these simple natures in their entirety; for if our intelligence puts itself in the least relation to them, which is necessary since we are supposed to make some sort of judgment about them, we must conclude from this that we know them in their entirety. Otherwise we could not say that it is simple, but rather that it is composed, first, of what we know about it, and second, of what we believe we do not know about it.

In the fourth place, we say that the connection of simple things with each other is necessary or contingent. It is necessary when the idea of one is so mixed with the idea of the other that, in wanting to judge them separately, it is impossible for us to conceive one of the two distinctly. It is in this way that the figure is linked to extent, the movement to duration or time, because it is impossible to conceive the figure deprived of extent, and the movement of duration. In the same way, when I say that four and three make seven, this connection is necessary, because one cannot conceive the number seven distinctly without including in it in a confused way the number four and the number three. In the same way, everything that is demonstrated about figures and numbers is necessarily linked to the thing about which the statement is made. This necessity does not only apply to sensible objects. For example, if Socrates says he doubts everything, it necessarily follows that he at least understands that he doubts; and that he knows that something can be true or false: for these are notions that necessarily accompany doubt. The connection is contingent when things are not inseparably linked together, for example when we say, the body is animate, the man is clothed. There are even many propositions which are necessarily joined together, and which the great number classify among the contingent ones, because one does not notice the relation of them: for example, I am, therefore God is; I understand, therefore I have a soul distinct from my body. Finally, it should be noted that there are a great number of necessary propositions, the reciprocal of which is contingent: thus, although, from what I am, I conclude with certainty that God is, I cannot reciprocally affirm, from what God is, that I exist.

We say, in the fifth place, that we cannot understand anything beyond these simple natures, and the compounds that are formed from them; and even it is often easier to examine several of them joined together than to abstract from one. Thus I can know a triangle without ever having noticed that this knowledge contains that of the angle, the line, the number three, the figure, the extent, etc.; which does not prevent us from saying that the nature of the triangle is a compound of all these natures, and that they are better known than the triangle, since they are the ones that we understand in it. There is more, in this same notion of the triangle, there are many others which are found there and which escape us, such as the size of the angles, which are equal to two rights, and the innumerable relations of the sides to the angles or to the capacity of the area.

In the sixth place, we say that the natures called composed are known to us because we find by experience that they are composed, or because we compose them ourselves. We know, for example, everything that we perceive by the senses, everything that we hear from others, and generally everything that comes to our understanding, either from elsewhere or from the reflective contemplation of the understanding by itself. It should be noted here that the understanding cannot be deceived by any experience, if it confines itself to the precise intuition of the object, as it possesses it in its idea or image. And let no one judge for this reason that the imagination represents faithfully the objects of the senses: the senses themselves do not reflect the true figure of things; and finally the external objects are not always such as they appear to us; we are in all these respects exposed to error, just as we can take a tale for a true story. A man afflicted with jaundice believes that everything is yellow, because his eye is of that color: a sick and melancholy mind may take for realities the vain phantoms of its imagination. But these same things will not mislead the intelligence of the wise man, because, while recognizing that what comes to him from the imagination has really been imprinted on it, he will never affirm that the notion has arrived unaltered from the external objects to the senses, and from the senses to the imagination, unless he has some other motive to be sure of it. On the other hand, it is we ourselves who compose the objects of our connoissance, whenever we believe that they contain something that our mind immediately perceives without any experience. Thus, when a man suffering from jaundice persuades himself that what he sees is yellow, his knowledge is composed both of what his imagination represents to him, and of what he derives from himself, namely, that the yellow color comes not from a defect in his eye, but from the fact that the things he sees are really yellow. It follows from all this that we can only be mistaken when we ourselves compose the notions we admit.

We say, in the seventh place, that this composition can be made in three ways, by impulse, by conjecture, or by deduction. Those who compose their judgments about things by impulse, who bring themselves to believe something without being persuaded by any reason, but only determined, either by a superior power, or by their own freedom, or by a disposition of their imagination. The first never deceives; the second, rarely; the third, almost always: but the first does not belong to this treatise, because it does not fall under the rules of art. The composition is made by conjecture when, for example, from the fact that water, further from the center of the earth, is also of a more tenuous substance; from the fact that air, placed above the earth, is also lighter than it, we conclude that beyond the air there is nothing but an ethereal substance, very pure, and much more tenuous than the air itself. The notions we form in this way do not deceive us, provided we take them only as probabilities, never as truths; but they do not make us more learned.

There remains, then, the only deduction by which we can compose notions of whose correctness we are sure; and yet a great many errors may still be made. For example, from the fact that in the air there is nothing that sight, touch or any other sense can grasp, we conclude that the space which encloses it is empty, we wrongly join the nature of emptiness to that of space; and this happens whenever we think we can deduce something general and necessary from a particular and contingent thing. But it is in our power to avoid this error, that is, never to make connections other than those which we have recognized as necessary: as, for example, when we conclude that nothing can be figured which is not extended, from the fact that the figure has a necessary relation to the extension.

From all this it follows, first of all, that we have clearly explained, and, it seems to me, by sufficient enumeration, what we were able to show at the beginning only confusedly and artlessly; namely, that there are only two ways open to man to arrive at a certain knowledge of truth, evident intuition and necessary deduction. We have moreover explained what these simple natures are, which are mentioned in the eighth rule. It is clear that intuition applies both to these natures, and to their necessary connection with each other, and finally to all other things which the understanding finds by precise experience, either in itself or in the imagination. As for deduction, we shall deal with it at greater length in the following rules.

Secondly, it follows that we need not take much trouble to know these simple natures, for they are sufficiently known by themselves. It is only necessary to distinguish them from one another, and to consider them carefully, successively and separately. Indeed, there is no one with such an obtuse mind who does not realize that there is some difference between sitting and standing. But not all of them distinguish so clearly the nature of the position from the other things contained in this idea, and they cannot affirm that in this case nothing is changed but the position. And we do not make this remark in vain, because scholars are usually ingenious enough to find ways of spreading darkness even in things which are obvious by themselves, and which the peasants are not ignorant of. This happens to them when they try to explain, by means of something more obvious, things that are known by themselves. For either they explain something else, or they explain nothing at all; for who does not know perfectly well the change of some kind that takes place when we change places, and what man will conceive the idea of this same change when he is told, The place is the surface of the surrounding body, since this surface can change while I remain immobile and do not change my place, and on the other hand move with me in such a way that, even though it is always the same that surrounds me, I am no longer in the same place? But does it not seem like magic words, which have a hidden virtue and are beyond the reach of the human mind, to say that movement (the thing best known to everyone) is the act of a power, as a power? Who understands these words, and who does not know what motion is? Who would not admit that this is looking for a knot in a piece of string? We must therefore recognize that we must never explain things of this kind by definitions, lest we mistake the simple for the compound, but only distinguish them from each other, and examine them carefully according to the lights of our mind.

Thirdly, it follows that all human science consists only in seeing distinctly how these simple natures contribute to the formation of other things, a remark which is very useful to make. For whenever a difficulty is proposed for examination, almost everyone stops at the beginning, uncertain of what thoughts they should first engage in, and convinced that they have to look for a new kind of being which is unknown to them. Thus, when they are asked what is the nature of a magnet, they immediately assume that the matter is difficult and arduous, and, distancing their minds from all that is obvious, they apply them to that which is most difficult, and wait in the dark to see if, by chance, in traversing the empty space of infinite causes, they will not find something new. But he who thinks that nothing can be found in the magnet that is not formed of certain simple natures and known by themselves, sure of what he must do, first gathers with care all the experiments he has on this stone, and then seeks to deduce from them what must be the necessary mixture of simple natures to produce the effects he has recognized in the magnet. Having found this, he can boldly state that he knows the true nature of the magnet, as much as a man with the given experiences can achieve.

Fourthly, it follows from what we have said that no one knowledge should be regarded as more obscure than another, since all are of the same nature, and consist only in the composition of things that are known by themselves: this is a truth to which few pay attention. But, warned of the contrary opinion, the most presumptuous allow themselves to give their conjectures as real demonstrations; and in things which they are completely ignorant of, they flatter themselves that they see hidden truths as through a cloud, and they are not afraid to put them forward, and wrap their conceptions in certain words, which serve them to discourse for a long time and to speak at length, but which in fact neither they nor their hearers understand. The most modest refrain from examining many things, sometimes very easy and very important for life, because they believe themselves incapable of reaching them; and as they think that they can be understood by other men endowed with more genius, they embrace the sentiment of those in whose authority they have the most confidence.

We say, in the eighth place, that one can only deduce things from words, the cause from the effect, the effect from the cause, the same from the same, or the parts or even the whole from the parts[2].....

Moreover, in order that no one may be mistaken about the sequence of our precepts, we divide everything that can be known into simple propositions and questions. For the simple propositions we shall give no other precepts than those which prepare the understanding to see distinctly and to study with sagacity all objects, because these propositions must present themselves spontaneously and cannot be sought. This is what we have done in our first twelve rules, in which we believe we have shown everything that, in our opinion, can facilitate the use of reason in some way. Among the questions, some are easily understood, even though their solution is unknown; these alone form the object of our next twelve rules: the others are not easily understood; we devote twelve other rules to them. This division has not been made without design; its purpose is to avoid saying anything that presupposes knowledge of what follows, and to instruct us first in what we consider to be a preliminary study necessary to the cultivation of the mind. It should be noted that, among the questions that are easily understood, we admit only those in which these three things are distinctly perceived, namely, by what signs can what we are looking for be recognized when it presents itself? from what precisely are we to deduce it? and how are we to prove that these two things depend so much on each other, that the one cannot change when the other does not change. Thus we shall have all our premises, and it will only remain for us to show how the conclusion is to be found, not by deducing any one thing from any one simple thing (for, as we have said, this is done without precept), but by so artfully disentangling one thing from a great number of others among which it is enveloped, that no greater capacity of mind is ever required than for the simplest conclusion. These questions, which are for the most part abstract and are found only in arithmetic and geometry, will seem of little use to those who are ignorant of these sciences; I warn them, however, that one must apply oneself for a long time and practice learning this method, if one wants to perfectly possess the second part of this treatise, where we will treat of all the other questions.

    rule thirteen.

When we understand a question perfectly, we must free it from any superfluous conception, reduce it to the simplest, subdivide it as much as possible by means of enumeration.

Here is the only point in which we imitate the dialecticians, and that is that, just as, to learn the forms of syllogisms, they suppose that the terms or the matter is known, so we require beforehand that the question be perfectly understood. But we don't distinguish, as they do, two extremes and a means : we consider the whole thing in this way. First, in every question it is necessary that there be something unknown, without which there would be no question. Secondly, this something must be designated in some way, otherwise there would be no reason to look for this thing rather than that thing. Thirdly, it can only be designated by something that is known. All this is found in even imperfect questions. Thus, when we ask what is the nature of a magnet, what is meant by these two words magnet and nature is known, and this is what determines us to look for that rather than something else. But, moreover, for the question to be perfect, we want it to be entirely determined, so that we seek nothing more than what can be deduced from the data: For example, if I am asked what is to be inferred about the nature of the magnet, precisely from the experiments which Gilbert says he has made, whether they are true or false; or again, if I am asked what I think about the nature of sound, precisely from the fact that the three strings a, b, c make an equal sound; b, in the hypothesis, being twice as large as a, of equal length, and stretched by twice the weight; and c being not larger than a, but twice as long, and stretched by four times the weight, etc. All these examples show how all imperfect questions can be reduced to perfect questions, which will be shown at greater length in its place; and moreover they teach in what way our rule can be observed when it commands us to free from all superfluous conception the difficulty well understood, and to reduce it to the point where we are no longer concerned with this or that object, but only, in general, with quantities to be compared with each other. For, for example, once we are determined to examine only this or that experiment on the magnet, we have no difficulty in distancing our thoughts from anything else.

It is added that one must reduce the difficulty to the simplest possible, according to rules five and six, and divide it according to rule seven. Thus, when I examine the magnet, according to several experiments, I go through them separately one after the other. In the same way, if I am dealing with sound, I compare separately the strings a and b, then a and c, and so on, and then embrace the whole in a sufficient enumeration. These are the only three rules that the intellect must observe for any proposition, before arriving at the final solution, even though it needs the following eleven rules, whose use will be explained in the third part of this treatise. Besides, we understand by questions all the things about which we find the truth and the falsehood; now, we must enumerate the various kinds of these questions, to determine what we can do about each one.

We have already said that falsity cannot be found in the mere intuition of things, whether simple or compound: in this sense, there is no question about these things; but they are a matter of question as soon as we want to make a certain judgment about them. Indeed, we do not only count as questions the requests made to us by others, but it was even a question that Socrates' ignorance, or rather doubt, when, for the first time, Socrates, reflecting, sought to know whether it was true that he doubted everything, and then affirmed it.

Now we look for things by words, causes by effects, effects by causes, the whole or parts by a part, or finally several things together by all of these.

We say that we look for things through words whenever the difficulty consists in the obscurity of language. Here are not only all the enigmas, like that of the Sphinx, about the animal which at first is quadruped, then biped, and finally walks on three feet; or that of the fishermen who, standing on the shore with their line and hooks, said that they no longer had the fish they had caught, but that on the other hand they had those they had not been able to catch. But, besides that, most of the questions on which scholars argue are almost always questions of words. Even one should not think so badly of great minds as to believe that they have imperfectly conceived things whenever they do not explain them in clear enough terms. Thus, when they call a place the surface of an ambient body, they do not have there a false idea, but only abuse the word place, which, in common usage, signifies that simple and self-evident nature, by reason of which something is said to be here or there, and which consists entirely in a certain relation of the thing which is said to be in a place, with the parts of extended space, and which some, seeing the name of place applied to an ambient surface, have improperly said to be the locality in itself[3] ; and so on. These questions of names occur so frequently, that if philosophers were always agreed on the meaning of words, almost all their controversies would cease.

We look for the cause by the effect every time we ask a thing if it is, or what it is[4].....

But because, when we are presented with a question to be solved, we do not suddenly notice what kind of question it is, nor whether it is a question of looking for the thing by the words, or the cause by the effect, it seems to me superfluous to enter here into more details; it will be shorter and easier to examine in order what we must do to arrive in general at the solution of any difficulty; and, consequently, a question being given, the first point is to endeavor to understand distinctly what we are looking for.

Indeed, most men are so hasty in their research that they bring to the solution of the question all the vagueness of a mind that has not noticed by what signs to recognize the thing sought, if it comes to be presented; as foolish as a servant sent somewhere by his master, and so eager to obey, that he begins to run without having yet received his orders, and without knowing where he must go.

But in any question, although there must be something unknown (for otherwise there would be no question), the thing sought must nevertheless be so designated by certain conditions that we are led to seek one thing rather than another. It is these conditions that we say we must first study; to do this, we must direct our mind to each of them in particular, examining carefully to what extent each determines this unknown thing we seek. For here the mind of man falls into a double error: either it takes to determine the question more than is given to it, or on the contrary it omits something.

We must beware of assuming more and something more positive than we have, especially in enigmas and in all the captious questions invented to embarrass the mind; and even in other questions, when in order to solve them we seem to admit as certain suppositions which are not given to us by positive reason, but by an opinion of habit. For example, in the enigma of the Sphinx, we must not believe that the word foot signifies only the real feet of the animals; we must also see if it does not apply metaphorically to something else, as here to the hands of the child, to the stick of the old man, because both of them use them as feet for walking. In the same way, in the enigma of the fishermen, we must be careful that the idea of fish takes hold of our mind so much that it distracts it from the thought of these animals which the poor often carry with them without wanting to, and which they reject when they have caught them. In the same way, if we ask how the vase was built, which we have sometimes seen, in the middle of which there is a column topped by the figure of Tantalus in the attitude of a man who wants to drink ; The water that was poured into it remained contained until it reached Tantalus' mouth, but no sooner did it touch the lips of the unfortunate man than it suddenly escaped entirely. At first glance, all the artifice seems to be in the construction of the figure of Tantalus, which however does not in any way determine the question, but only accompanies it. The whole difficulty consists in finding out how a vase can be constructed in such a way that all the water escapes from it as soon as it has reached a certain height, and not before. Finally, if from all the observations that we have on the stars we seek what we can affirm of certainty about their movements, we must not gratuitously admit that the earth is immobile at the center, as the ancients did, because from our childhood it has seemed to us to be so; but we must revoke this very assertion, in order to examine afterwards what we can judge of certainty on this subject.

We sin by omission whenever we do not reflect on some condition required for the determination of the question, whether it is expressed therein, or whether it can be recognized in some way. Thus do those who seek perpetual motion, not that of nature, of the stars or springs, for example, but a motion created by human art, a discovery that many have believed possible. Calculating that the earth is perpetually moved in a circular motion around its axis, and that the magnet retains the properties of the earth, they hoped to discover perpetual motion by arranging this stone in such a way that it would move in a circle, or at least communicate to the iron its motion with its other virtues. But when they succeeded in doing this, they would not yet have found perpetual motion. They would only have made use of the one given to them by nature, just as if they had arranged a wheel in the current of a river so that it would always turn. This is to omit a necessary condition for the determination of the question.

The question being sufficiently understood, it is necessary to see precisely in what its difficulty consists, so that abstracted from all the rest, it is more easily solved.

It is not always enough to understand the question in order to know what its difficulty consists of; it is necessary to reflect in addition on each of the things it contains, so that if we come across something easy to find, we leave it aside, and that only what we do not know remains of the question thus cleared up. Thus, in the question of the vase described above, it is easy to see how the vase should be made, the column placed in the middle, the bird painted; all this put aside as not being important to the question, the difficulty remains naked, which consists in seeking why the water previously contained in a vase, escapes from it entirely when it has reached a certain height.

We are therefore content here to say that it is important to go through in order all that is contained in the given question, rejecting what we see is not useful, keeping what is necessary, and postponing what is doubtful to a more careful examination.

rule fourteen.

The same rule must apply to the real extent of bodies, and it must be represented entirely to the imagination, by means of naked figures; in this way the understanding will understand it much more distinctly.

To make use of the help of the imagination, we must note that whenever we deduce an unknown thing from something that was known to us before, we do not find a new being, but only the knowledge that we possessed is extended to the point of making us understand that the thing sought participates in some way in the nature of the things that the data contain. Thus we must not hope to be able to give a man born blind true ideas about colors, as we have received them from the senses. But let there be a man who has sometimes seen the fundamental colors, and never the intermediate and mixed colors; it may be that by a sort of deduction he will represent those he has not seen, by their resemblance to the others. In the same way, if the magnet contains a kind of being to which our intelligence has not yet perceived anything similar, we must not hope that reasoning will make us know it; we would need either new senses or a divine soul. But all that the human mind can do in this case, we shall believe we have achieved when we have distinctly perceived the mixture of beings or matters already known, which produce the same effects that the magnet develops.

Now, all the beings already known, such as extent, figure, motion, and so many others, which it is not the place here to enumerate, are, in the various subjects, known by one and the same idea; and whether a crown is of gold or silver, it changes nothing in the idea we have of its figure. This general idea passes from one subject to another by a simple comparison, by which we affirm that the object sought is in such and such a respect similar, identical, or equal to a given thing; so that, in all reasoning, we know the truth precisely only by comparison. Thus, in this reasoning, all A is B, all B is C, so all A is C, we compare together the thing sought and the thing given A and C, in this respect, namely that A and C are B. But since, as we have often repeated, forms and syllogisms are of no use in discovering the truth of things, the reader will profit, if, rejecting them completely, he persuades himself that all connoissance which does not come from the pure and simple intuition of an individual object derives from the comparison of two or more with each other; and even almost all the industry of human reason consists in preparing for this operation: when indeed the comparison is simple and clear, there is no need of any help from art, but only from the light of nature, to perceive the truth which it discovers to us. Now, it should be noted that comparisons are said to be simple and clear only when the thing sought and the thing given participate equally in a certain nature; that other comparisons need no preparation except because this common nature is not found equally in one and the other, but according to the ratios or proportions in which it is wrapped; and that finally the greater part of human industry consists only in reducing these proportions to such an extent that the equality between what is sought and something that is known appears clearly.

It should then be noted that nothing can be reduced to this equality but what comprises the plus or the minus, and that all this is understood under the name of magnitude; so that when, according to the preceding rule, the terms of the difficulty are abstracted from any subject, we understand that the whole question is only about magnitudes in general.

But in order to imagine something else here, and to make use not of pure intelligence, but of intelligence aided by figures painted in the imagination, let us notice that nothing is said about magnitudes in general that cannot be related to each of them in particular.

From this it is easy to conclude that it will not be of little use to us to transfer what we know of magnitudes in general to that particular kind of magnitude which will be represented most easily and most distinctly in our imagination.

Now that this magnitude is the real extent of a body, abstracted from everything that is not the figure, this is what follows from what we said in the twelfth rule, where we showed that the imagination itself, with the ideas that exist in it, is nothing other than the real body, extended and figured; which is evident by itself, since all the differences of position do not appear more distinctly in any other subject. Indeed, although we can say of one thing that it is more or less white than another, of a sound that it is more or less acute, and so on, we cannot however exactly define whether this excess is in double or triple proportion, except by some analogy to the extent of the body represented. Let it therefore remain certain and settled that perfectly determined questions contain hardly any other difficulty than that of finding the proportional measure of inequality; that all things in which there is precisely such a difficulty can easily and must be separated from any other subject, and transported to the extent and figures, which for this reason we shall deal with exclusively up to the twenty-fifth rule, leaving aside all other thoughts.

I would like here a reader who has a taste only for mathematical and geometrical studies, although I would rather he was not versed in them at all than instructed according to the vulgar method. Indeed, the use of the rules which I will give here, and which suffice to learn them, is much easier than in any other kind of question, and their usefulness is so great for acquiring a higher science, that I am not afraid to say that this part of our method was not invented to solve mathematical problems, but rather that mathematics must be learned only to practice this method. I will only assume from these studies what is known by oneself and presents itself to each one. But the knowledge that others have of it, even though it is not spoiled by any obvious error, is nevertheless obscured by equivocal and ill-conceived principles, which we will try to correct as we come across them.

We understand by extent everything that has length, breadth and depth, without investigating whether it is a real body or only a space; and this needs no further explanation, since there is nothing that our imagination perceives more easily. But as scholars often use distinctions so subtle that they confuse natural lights, and find darkness even in things that peasants have never been ignorant of, they must be warned that by extent we do not designate anything distinct or separate from a subject, and that in general we do not recognize any of the philosophical beings of this kind, which do not really fall under the imagination. For even though someone may persuade himself that, by annihilating all that is extended in nature, there is nothing to deny that extension alone exists by itself, he will not use a corporeal idea for this conception, but only his own false intelligence. He will recognize this himself, provided he thinks carefully about the very image of extent that he will then try to picture in his imagination. He will indeed notice that he does not perceive it apart from any subject, but that he imagines it quite differently from the way he judges it: in such a way that all these abstract beings, whatever opinion the intelligence may have about the truth of the thing, are never formed in the imagination apart from any subject.

But, as from now on we will do nothing without the help of the imagination, we must carefully distinguish under which idea each word must present itself to our intelligence. So we propose to examine these three ways of speaking: extent occupies the place, every body has extent, extent is not the body. The first shows how extent is taken to be what is extended; indeed, I conceive the same thing when I say that extent occupies the place, as if I were to say that an extended being occupies the place. And it does not follow, however, that it would be better, to avoid equivocation, to use the word extended being; it would not express as distinctly the idea that we conceive, namely, that a subject occupies the place because it is extended; and perhaps it could be understood that the extended being is a subject that occupies the place, just as when I say that an animated being occupies the place. This explains why we preferred to say that we would deal with extension (extensione), rather than with extended being (de extenso), even though we think that the former should not be understood otherwise than as extended being. Let us pass to these words, every body has extent; where we understand that extent means something other than body, without however forming in our imagination two distinct ideas, one of a body, the other of extent, but simply one, that of an extended body: basically it is as if I were to say, every body is extended, or rather, what is extended is extended. And this is a character peculiar to everything that exists only in another, and can never be conceived without a subject, a character that is not found in that which is really distinct from the subject. Thus, when I say, Peter has wealth, the idea of Peter is quite different from that of wealth; similarly, when I say, Paul is rich, I imagine something quite different from when I say the rich man is rich. Failing to make this difference, most people falsely imagine that extent contains something distinct from what is extended, just as Paul's riches are something other than Paul. Finally, if we say, extent is not a body, the word extent is taken in a completely different way than above, and in this sense no idea corresponds to it in the imagination. But this statement is made entirely by the pure intelligence, which alone has the faculty of distinguishing abstract beings of this kind. This is a cause of error for many people. For, without noticing that extent taken in this sense cannot be imagined, they represent to themselves a real idea of it, and this idea necessarily implying the conception of a body, if they say that extent thus conceived is not a body, they get into trouble without knowing it in this proposition, that the same thing is at the same time a body and is not one. Therefore it is of great importance to distinguish statements in which names of this kind, extent, figure, number, surface, line, point, unit, have such an exact meaning that they exclude something from which, in reality, they are not distinct; for example, when we say the extent or the figure is not a body, the number is not the thing counted, the surface is the limit of a body, the line of the surface, the point of the line, the unit is not a quantity; all propositions which must be far from the imagination, whatever their truth; so we shall not deal with them in the following. It must be carefully observed that in all other propositions in which these names, while retaining the same meaning and being employed without regard to any subject, do not exclude or deny a thing of which they are not really distinct, we can and must avail ourselves of the help of the imagination, because, even though the intellect only pays attention to what the word designates, the imagination must nevertheless imagine a true image of the thing, so that, if it is necessary, the intellect can refer to the other conditions which the word does not express, and does not imprudently believe that they have been excluded. If it is a question of numbers, we shall imagine a subject of some kind, measurable by several units, and, although the intellect at present reflects only on the plurality, we must be careful that in the future it does not conclude something that makes us suppose that the thing counted was excluded from our conception; as do those who attribute to numbers mysterious properties, pure frivolities, to which they would not attribute so much faith if they did not conceive of number as distinct from the things counted. In the same way, if we deal with the figure, we shall think that we are dealing with an extended subject, conceived in this respect that it is figured: if of a body, we must think that we are examining it as long, broad, and deep; if of a surface, as long and broad, apart from the depth, but without denying it; if of a line, as long only; if of a point, we shall abstract all other characters, except that it is a being. All this is here very well developed; but men have so many prejudices in their minds, that I am still afraid that only a few are here safe from error, and that the explanation of my thought will be found too short in spite of the length of the speech. Indeed, arithmetic and geometry themselves, although the most certain of all the sciences, nevertheless deceive us in this respect. Who is the calculator who does not believe that he must not only abstract his numbers from any subject by intelligence, but also really distinguish them by imagination? What geometer does not obscure the evidence of his object in spite of the principles, when he judges that lines have no width, nor surfaces depth, and that after that he composes them one with the other, without thinking that this line whose movement he conceives to generate a surface, is a real body, and that the one on the contrary which lacks width is nothing but a modification of the body, etc.? But, in order not to dwell too long on these observations, it will be shorter to explain in what way we suppose our object must be conceived, in order to demonstrate in this respect as easily as possible all that arithmetic and geometry contain of truths.

We are therefore concerned here with an extended object, without considering in it anything other than the extent itself, and purposely abstaining from the word quantity, because philosophers are subtle enough to distinguish also quantity from extent. We suppose that all the questions have come to the point where all that remains to be sought is a certain extent, which we shall know by comparing it with another already known extent. Indeed, since here we do not expect to know any new being, but only to bring the propositions, however awkward they may be, to the point where the unknown is found equal to something known, it is certain that all the differences of proportion that exist in other subjects can also be found between two or more extents. And consequently it is sufficient for our purpose to consider in the extent itself all the elements which can help to expose the differences of proportions, elements which are only three in number: the dimension, the unit, the figure.

By dimension we mean nothing else than the mode and manner in which any object is considered measurable; so that not only length, breadth, and depth are dimensions of bodies, but also gravity is the dimension according to which objects are weighed; speed, the dimension of motion: and so on. The division itself into several equal parts, whether real or intellectual, is properly the dimension according to which we count things; and this mode which makes the number is, properly speaking, a kind of dimension, though there is some diversity in the meaning of the word. Indeed, if we consider the parts in relation to the whole, we are said to be counting; if, on the contrary, we consider the whole as divided into parts, we measure it: for example, we measure the centuries by the years, the days, the hours, the moments; if, on the contrary, we count the moments, the days, the years, we will end up completing the centuries.

It follows from this that in one and the same object there can be infinitely diverse dimensions, that they add absolutely nothing to the things that possess them, but that they must be understood in the same way, whether they have a real foundation in the objects themselves, or whether they have been arbitrarily invented by our mind. Indeed, it is something real that the weight of a body, the speed of motion, or the division of the century into years and days: but it is not the same for the division of the day into hours and moments. However, all these things are equal if we consider them only from the point of view of dimension, as we must do here and in mathematics. Indeed, it is rather for physics to examine whether the basis of these divisions is real or not.

This consideration sheds a great light on geometry, because in this science almost everyone will wrongly conceive of three kinds of quantities, the line, the surface and the body. We reported above that line and surface do not fall under the conception, as truly distinct from the body, or from each other; if, on the contrary, we consider them simply as abstracted by the intelligence, there are no more different kinds of quantity than there are different kinds of substance in man, being animate and living. It should be noted in passing that the three dimensions of bodies, length, breadth and depth, differ only in name from one another. Indeed, nothing prevents us from taking any one of the three extents for length, the other for width, etc., in a given solid. And although these three things only have a real foundation in any extended object, as extended, yet we are no more concerned with them here than with so many others, which either are fictions of the intelligence, or have other foundations in things. Thus, in a triangle, when one wants to measure it exactly, three things are to be known on the side of the object, that is, the three sides, or two sides and an angle, or two angles and the area, etc.; in the same way, in a trapezoid, five data are needed, six in a tetrahedron, etc. All this can be called dimensions; but in order to choose those which help our imagination the most, we must never embrace more than one or two of those which are in our imagination, even if we see that in the proposition which occupies us there are several others. The art, in fact, consists in dividing them up as much as possible, and in directing our attention to a small number at a time, but nevertheless successively to all of them.

Unity is that common nature in which, as I have said above, all things that are compared with each other must participate equally. And if in the question there is not already a determined unit, we can take in its place, either one of the sizes already given, or any other; it will be the measure of all the others. In this unit we put as many dimensions as in the extremes, which will have to be compared between them; we conceive it then, either simply as something extended, disregarding all other things (and then it will be identical to the point of the geometers, when they compose the line by its movement), or as a line, or as the square.

As for figures, it has been shown above how it is by them alone that one can form ideas of all things. It remains to warn here that, in the diversity of their innumerable kinds, we shall only use those which express most easily all the differences of ratios or proportions. Now there are only two things that we can compare with each other, quantities and magnitudes; we also have two kinds of figures suitable for representing them: thus the points

Now, to show what principles we shall use in all this, we must know that all the relations that can exist between beings of the same kind are reduced to two, order and measure. One must also know that it takes no little art to find order, as can be seen in this method, which teaches almost nothing else. As for knowing the order once we have found it, there is no difficulty there; we can very easily, according to rule seven, bring our mind to each of the ordered parts; because, in this kind of relationship, the ones refer to the others by themselves, and not through the intermediary of a third, as happens in measurements, which for this reason we are dealing with exclusively here. I do indeed recognize that order exists between A and B, without considering anything other than the two extremes; but I do not recognize what the proportion of magnitude is between two and three, unless I consider a third term, namely unity, which is the common measure of the one and the other.

Moreover, it is necessary to know that continuous quantities can, with the help of the assumed unit, sometimes be reduced to a plurality, and always at least in part; and that the multitude of units can be arranged in such a way that the difficulty, which belongs to the knowledge of measurement, depends only on the inspection of the order, a progress in which art is of great help

Finally, it is necessary to know that, among the dimensions of a continuous size, we do not conceive of any more distinctly than length and width; that we should not pay attention to several at the same time in the same figure, but only to two that are different from each other; because if we have to compare more than two that are not similar, art requires that we go through them successively, and that we observe only two at a time.

This being the case, it is easy to conclude that we must abstract the proportions from the very figures that geometers deal with, when it comes to them, as well as from any other matter. For this purpose we must keep only rectangular and rectilinear surfaces, and straight lines, which we also call figures, because they serve us no less than surfaces to represent a truly extended subject, as I have already said; finally, by these lines we must represent sometimes continuous magnitudes, sometimes plurality and number, and human industry can find nothing simpler to expose all the differences in relationships.

rule fifteen.

Often it is good to draw these figures, and to show them to the external senses, to keep our mind more easily attentive.

It is self-evident how they should be drawn, so that at the moment they strike our eyes their figure is represented in our imagination. We can paint the unit in three ways, by a square , if we consider it as long and wide; by a line -, if we consider it only as long; and finally by a point . if we consider it only as a plurality. But, in whatever way we represent it and conceive it, we will always understand that it is a subject extended in all directions, and capable of an infinity of dimensions. In the same way, we shall represent to the eye the terms of a proposition, when it is necessary to examine at once the various magnitudes of it, by a rectangle in which two sides will be the two proposed magnitudes, in this way , if they are commensurable with the unit; or in this other

or this one , if they are commensurable, without adding anything, unless it is a question of a multitude of units. If finally we examine only one of their magnitudes, we will represent the line either by the rectangle , one side of which will be the proposed magnitude, and the other the unit in this way , which is done each time the same line is to be compared with any surface; or by the line alone -, if we consider it to be an incommensurable length; or in this way ... . . if it is a multitude of units.

rule sixteen.

As for what does not require the attention of the mind, though necessary for the conclusion, it is better to designate it by short notes than by whole figures. In this way memory will not fail us, and yet the mind will not be distracted, in order to retain it, from the other operations with which it is occupied.

Moreover, as we have said that, among the innumerable dimensions that can be imagined in our imagination, we cannot embrace more than two at a time, with one and the same glance, either of the eyes or of the mind, it is good to retain all the others accurately enough so that they can present themselves to us whenever we need them. It is for this purpose that nature seems to have given us memory; but as it is often subject to failure, and in order not to be obliged to give part of our attention to renewing it, while we are occupied with other thoughts, art has very appropriately invented writing, with the help of which, without handing over anything to our memory, and abandoning our imagination freely and without division to the ideas which occupy it, we entrust to paper what we want to retain, and this by means of short notes, so that after having examined each thing separately, according to the ninth rule, we can, according to the eleventh rule, go through them all by the rapid movement of thought, and embrace at once the greatest number possible.

Thus everything that must be considered as a unit, for the solution of the question, we will designate it by a single note, which can be taken arbitrarily. But to make it easier, we will use the characters a, b, c, etc., to express the quantities already known, and A, B, C, for the unknown quantities, which we will precede by the figures 1, 2, 3, 4, etc., to indicate their number, and follow by the same figures to express the number of relations they contain. For example, if I write 2 a3, it is as if I were saying, the double of the magnitude represented by a, which contains three ratios. By this means, not only will we save words, but also, and this is very important, we will present the terms of the difficulty so bare and so uncluttered, that even if we do not forget anything useful, we will nevertheless leave nothing superfluous, and which occupies in vain the capacity of our mind when it has to embrace several things at once.

To make all this clearer, notice first that calculators are accustomed to designate each magnitude by several units, or by any number, whereas we are not disregarding numbers here any less than we did earlier with regard to the figures of geometry or any other thing whatsoever. We do this in order to avoid the tedium of a long and superfluous calculation, and mainly to leave always distinct the parts of the subject in which the difficulty consists, without enveloping them in useless numbers. Thus, if we look for the base of a right-angled triangle, whose sides are 9 and 12, a calculator will say that it is 225 or 15. For us, instead of 9 and 12, we will put a and b, and we will find that the base is 2+2 ; thus will remain distinct these two parts, a and b, which in the number are confused.

It should then be noted that, by number of relations, one must understand the proportions which follow one another in continuous order, proportions which in common algebra one tries to express by several dimensions and figures, and of which one calls the first root, the second square, the third cube, the fourth square square, words which, I confess, have long deceived me. It seemed to me that nothing could be clearer to my imagination, after the line and the square, than the cube and other similar figures. They even served me to solve a good number of difficulties; but finally, after many experiments, I realized that I had found nothing by this way of conceiving that I could not have recognized more easily and more distinctly without it; that it was finally necessary to reject all these names, for fear that they might disturb our conception, for the reason that the same size, whether it is called a cube or a square, must never, however, according to the preceding rule, present itself to our imagination as anything but a line or a surface. It should be noted first of all that the root, the square, the cube, are only magnitudes in continuous proportion, which are always assumed to be preceded by this borrowed unit we have already mentioned. It is to this unit that the first proportional relates immediately, and by a single relation; the second, which has as its intermediary the first, by two relations; the third, which has as its intermediary the first and the second, by three relations; we shall therefore henceforth call the first proportional the quantity which, in algebra, bears the name of root; the second proportional, the square; and so on.

Finally, let us notice that, although we believe we must here abstract from certain numbers the terms of the difficulty in order to examine its nature, it often happens that it could have been solved more simply with the numbers given, than free from these numbers. This is because of the double use of numbers, of which we have already touched on something; that is, the same numbers explain sometimes the order, sometimes the measure. And so, after having sought the solution of the difficulty when this difficulty is expressed in general terms, we must recall it to the given numbers, to see if by chance they would not themselves give us a simpler solution. For example, having seen that the base of a right-angled triangle whose sides are a and b was $2+2$, that for a2 we should place 81, and for b2 144, which, added together, make 225, whose root or proportional mean between unity and 225 is 15 ; we conclude that the base 15 is commensurable with the sides 9 and 12, not generally because it is the base of a right-angled triangle, of which one of the sides is to the other as 3 to 4. All this we distinguish, we who seek to have a clear and definite knowledge of things; but the calculators do not worry about it, being content to find the sum sought, without noticing how it depends on the data, the one and only point in which science consists.

Finally, it should be observed in general that we should not entrust to our memory anything that does not require perpetual attention, if it can be put down on paper, lest this superfluous recollection should rob a part of our mind of the thought of the present object. We must draw up a table to write down the terms of the question, as it was proposed the first time; then we will indicate how they are abstracted, and by what signs they are represented, so that, when the signs themselves have given us the solution, we can apply it without any help from our memory to the particular subject; indeed, one thing can only be abstracted from another less general one. I will therefore write in this way: we are looking for the base A, C in the right-angled triangle A, B, C; and I abstract the difficulty to look in general for the size of the base according to the size of the sides; then, instead of ab, which equals 9, instead of bc, which equals 12, I put b. and so on.

It should be noted, moreover, that these four rules will be used again in the third part of this treatise, but taken in a greater latitude than here, as will be said in its place.

rule seventeen.

It is necessary to go directly through the proposed difficulty, disregarding the fact that some of its terms are known and the others unknown, and following, by the true course, the mutual dependence of the one and the other.

The last four rules have taught us how determined and perfectly understood difficulties must be abstracted from each subject, and reduced to the point where there is nothing left to search for but a few quantities that we will know, because they relate in this or that way to certain data. Now we shall set forth in the following five rules how these difficulties are to be treated, so that all the unknown quantities contained in a proportion are subordinated to one another, and that the rank which the first occupies with respect to the unit, the second occupies with respect to the first, the third with respect to the second, the fourth with respect to the third, and so on, if the number goes further, so that they add up to a known quantity; and all this by a method so certain, that we can surely affirm that no other method could have reduced it to simpler terms.

But for the present, we must notice that, in any question to be solved by deduction, there is a simple and direct way by which we can pass from one term to another with the greatest ease, while all the other ways are indirect and more difficult. To understand this, we need only recall what we said in Rule XI, where we explained the sequence of propositions, which, when compared in isolation, each with the one nearest to it, let us easily see how the first and the last are related, although we cannot so easily deduce the intermediates from the extremes. Now, if we consider the dependence of each one on the other, without the order being interrupted anywhere, in order to conclude from this how the last one depends on the first one, we are directly traversing the difficulty. But on the contrary, if, from what we know that the first and the last are joined together by some connection, we wanted to deduce the intermediaries that unite them, it would be to follow an indirect path that is contrary to natural order. But since here we are dealing only with questions that are wrapped up, in which we must discover by a reverse procedure, the extremes[5] being known, certain intermediate terms, the whole art in this place must be to be able, by supposing known what is not known, to provide ourselves with an easy and direct means of research even in the most embarrassing difficulties; and there is nothing to prevent this from always taking place, since we assumed at the beginning of this part that we recognize that the unknown terms in the question are in mutual dependence on the known terms, so that they are perfectly determined by them. If, then, we reflect on the things that first appear to us as soon as we recognize this determination, and we put them, though unknown, among the things that are known, in order to deduce from them, gradually and by the true route, the known itself as if it were unknown, we shall fulfill all that this rule requires. We will leave the examples of this and other things we have to talk about to the twenty-fourth rule, because that is where they belong.

rule eighteen.

For this, only four operations are needed, addition, subtraction, multiplication and division; even the last two often don't need to be done, both to avoid embracing anything unnecessarily, and because they can then be more easily performed.

The multiplicity of rules often comes from the ignorance of the masters, and what could be reduced to a single general principle is less clear when divided into several particular rules. We therefore reduce under four heads only all the operations we need to go through the questions, that is, to deduce the quantities from one another. How is this number sufficient? This is what the explanation of this rule will show.

Indeed, if we come to know a quantity because we have the parts of which it is composed, this is done by addition; if we know a part because we have the whole and the excess of the whole over the part, this is done by subtraction. There is no other way to deduce any quantity from other quantities taken absolutely, and in which it is contained in any way. If, on the other hand, a quantity is intermediate between others, from which it is entirely distinct and which do not contain it at all, it must be related to them by some point; and this relationship, if it is directly sought, will be found by multiplication; if it is indirectly, by division.

To clarify these two things, we must know that the unit, which we have already spoken of, is here the basis and foundation of all relationships, and that in a series of quantities in continuous proportion it occupies the first degree; that the given quantities are in the second degree; that in the third, fourth and others are the quantities sought if the proportion is direct; if on the contrary it is indirect, the unknown is in the second degree and in the intermediate degrees, and the known in the last. For if we say, as the unit is a or 5, a given number, so b or 7, a given number, is in the unknown, which is ab or 35, then a and b are in the second degree, and ab, which is the product of them, is in the third; if we add, as the unit is c or 9, so ab or 35 is in the unknown abc or 315, then abc is in the fourth degree, and the product of two multiplications of ab and c which are in the second degree, and so of the rest. Similarly, as the unit is at $a = 5$, so $a = 5$ is at $a2$ or 25; and on the other hand, as the unit is at $a = 5$, so $a2$ or 25 is at $a3$ or 125; and finally, as the unit is at $a = 5$, so $a3 = 125$ is $a4$ which equals 625, etc. Indeed, multiplication is not done otherwise, whether one multiplies the same quantity by itself, or multiplies it by another which differs entirely from it.

Now if we say: as the unit is $a = 5$, given divisor, so B or 7 unknown is to ab or 35, given dividend, the order is reversed. Also B unknown can only be found by dividing ab by a given also; similarly if we say, as the unit is to a or 5 unknown, so a or 5 unknown is to $A2$ or 25 given, or as the unit is to $A = 5$ unknown, so $A2$ or 25 sought, is to $A3$ or 125 given, and so on. We include all these operations under the heading of division, although it should be noted that the latter species contain more difficulties than the former, because often the quantity sought is contained in them, which consequently contains more ratios. For these examples amount to saying that one must extract the square root of $a2$ or 25, or the cube of $a3$ or 125, and so on. This way of expressing oneself, used among the calculators, is equivalent, to use the expressions of the geometers, to this form, that it is necessary to seek the proportional average, between this quantity from which one starts, and which we name unit, and that which we designate by $a2$, or the two proportional averages between the unit and a3, and so on.

From this, we can easily understand how these two operations are sufficient to find all the quantities which, by some relation, must be deduced from certain others. Having understood this, it remains for us to explain how these operations must be brought to the examination of the imagination, and how they must be shown to the eyes, in order to explain their use and practice.

If it is a question of making a division, or a subtraction, we conceive of the subject in the form of a line or an extended magnitude in which we must consider only the length. For if we have to add the line a to the line b, we will join the one to the other in this way , and we will have . If, on the other hand, we must extract the smaller from the larger, for example b from a, we apply them to each other in this way, , and we have the part of the larger that the smaller cannot cover, namely . In multiplication we shall also have these large data in the form of lines; but we imagine that they form a rectangle, for if we multiply a by b, we adopt our two lines at right angles ab in this way , and we have the rectangle

Moreover, if we want to multiply by , we must conceive ab as a line, namely , to have

for abc.

Finally, in the division where the divisor is given, we imagine that the size to be divided is a rectangle, one of whose sides is divisor and the other quotient. So either the rectangle has to divide by , we remove the width and we have for quotient, or on the contrary if we divide by we will remove the width and the quotient will be .

But in divisions where the divisor is not given, but only indicated by some ratio, as when we say that we must extract the square or cubic root, etc., we must then conceive the dividend and all the other terms, as lines existing in a series of continuous proportions, the first of which is the unit, and the last the quantity to be divided; to the rest, how it will be necessary to find between this last and the unit all the proportional averages, is what will be said in its place. It is sufficient to warn that we assume that such operations have not yet been completed here, since they can only take place by a reverse and reflective direction of the imagination, and that we are dealing here only with operations that are done directly.

As for the other operations, they are very easy to do, in the way we have said that they must be conceived. It remains, however, to explain how the terms are to be prepared; for, although at the first appearance of a difficulty we are free to conceive the terms, as lines or rectangles, without ever attributing to them other figures, as was said in rule xiv, often however, in the course of the operation the rectangle once produced by the multiplication of two lines must soon be conceived as a line for the use of another operation, or the same rectangle, or the line produced by an addition or subtraction, must be conceived as another rectangle indicated above the line by which it is to be divided.

It is therefore necessary to explain here how any rectangle can be transformed into a line, and, on the other hand, the line or even the rectangle into another rectangle, the side of which is designated; this is very easy for geometers if they notice that by lines, whenever we compare them, as here, with a rectangle, we always conceive of rectangles, one side of which is the length that we have taken as the unit. Thus everything reduces to this proposition: Given a rectangle, construct another equal one on a given side.

Although this operation is familiar to those less advanced in geometry, I will nevertheless explain it so as not to appear to have forgotten anything.

nineteenth rule.

It is by this method that we must look for as many quantities expressed in two different ways as we suppose to be known by unknown terms, in order to go directly through the difficulty; because, by this means, we will have as many comparisons between two equal things.

twentieth rule.

After having found the equations, we must complete the operations that we have omitted, without ever using multiplication whenever there is a need for division.

(The rest is missing)

rule twenty-one.

If there are several equations of this kind, they must all be reduced to one, namely to the one whose terms will occupy the smallest number of degrees in the series of quantities in continuous proportion, according to which these terms themselves must be arranged.

Afterword by the Translator

The Philosopher of Skeptical Rationalism: Rational Metaphysics and the Kernel of Nominalism

Rene Descartes, usually known by his Latin moniker Cartesius (hence, "Cartesian"), aimed to replace the syllogistic reasoning with a new method that he developed, in part sparked from his philosophy of mathematics. His method was characterized by its simplicity and aimed to avoid error by using a systematic approach to thinking. Descartes believed that this new method would provide a more reliable way of acquiring knowledge than the scholastic method that had been taught in universities. This method of clear reasoning and rational doubting was instrumental in the enlightenment, which he introduced methodically in his 1641 "Meditations on First Philosophy". This method involved systematically doubting everything he believed to be true in order to arrive at indubitable knowledge. His famous 1637 Discourse on Method is a foundation work of this process towards true knowledge: "I was convinced that I must once and for all undertake to rid myself of all the opinions which I had formerly accepted, and to begin anew from the very foundations, if I wanted to establish anything firm and lasting in the sciences."

He famously concluded that the only thing he could be sure of was his own existence, which he expressed in the phrase "Cogito, ergo sum" ("I think, therefore I am"). This idea helped establish the importance of the individual, the univocally of the Subject, in philosophy and paved the way for the Enlightenment. Hegel summarized Descartes this way:

> <u>The course of Descartes is the course of the clear understanding.</u> Certainty is the first thing; content is not necessarily derived from it, neither content at all, still less its objectivity as distinguished from the inner subjectivity of the ego. But it is said that we find in ourselves the idea of the most perfect; the idea is here presupposed as found. By this is measured the mere idea of God, which contains no existence in itself; and it is found that without existence it would be imperfect. This unity of God himself, of his idea with his existence, is, however, the truthfulness; by this we have just as much reason to hold true that which is as certain for us as the truth of ourselves.

Descartes' methods still constitute the foundation of mathematics. His simple Cartesian Coordinate System is known by anyone with a high school level of education- every graph with an X and Y axis we see daily has their origin in Descates. His method of doubt became an important tool in the development of modern scientific methodology in both the "hard" and "soft" science. Descartes' sign rule is used in mathematics today- like Sturm's chain - to determine the maximum number of positive and negative zeros of a real polynomial. His work was the foundation that Leibnitz and Newton used to create Calculus.

He created analytic geometry through the Cartesian coordinate system, which allows for the plotting of points on a graph using two perpendicular axes. He made important contributions to Physics, Optics and Astronomy. He wrote in his early Geometry; "I thus hope that geometry, which has long been added to philosophy, will provide its students with a more certain method, and more easily understood proofs, than any of the other parts of mathematics."

His contribution to mathematics is ironic because he doubts the very veracity of mathematics. While he was first and foremost a mathematician before he is a philosopher, Descartes' philosophy of skepticism threw into doubt even science. Because since the set of all possible integers is infinite, the set of constructible addition problems is also infinite, meaning the truth of mathematics can never be demonstrated fully. So even his beloved mathematics could not be a source of truth, a 0:0 on the X-Y axis he invented. The rules of the universe, Descartes realized, are only patterns that we have not seen broken yet.

Arriving at his own consciousness as the only knowable, certain truth, he inverts the proofs of the existence of God, and subsequently math, separating himself from both Materialists and the Theologians of his day. His philosophic movement is this: if his only source of absolute knowledge is that he is, then there are certain correlatives associated with this knowledge of the existence of the self, including that he is fallible, weak, and finite. And through the principle of correlatives- that there can be no true without false, no North without South etc, then there must be a being which is on the opposite side of himself on this spectrum – infinite, originless and all powerful. Instead of deriving man from God, Descartes derives God from himself. This is quite similar to Plato's divided line, where he also validates mathematics through the existence of God, the supreme good.

Despite his best efforts to save his work from the same fate as his contemporary Galileo, Descartes' ideas came under fire from both the Catholic Church and Protestant churches, which placed his works on the Index of Forbidden Books in 1663. Ironically, he is often accused of Theism from the Modernist and Empiricist anti-metaphysical thinkers like Hume and Nietzsche due to his Platonic Mind-Body dichotomy and opposition to pure Newtonian Mechanical Reductionism. He both founded Metaphysics and planted the Kernel of Subjectivity found in the Reformation's Nominalism, which would be the death of Metaphysics as well. Cartesian philosophy is deeply Tautological, hence the thousand different readings from thinkers, even those within the same camp. The great Atheist thinker Schopenhauer loved Descartes, while the arch-atheist Nietzsche hated him. C.S. Lewis had great respect for Descartes, while Pascal thought he was the source of everything wrong in the world. The intricacy of his metaphysics lends itself to this kaleidoscopic interpretation.

Speculative Skepticism: Platonic Ontology Clashing against Materialism

Descartes' commitment to reason and clear thinking also led him to reject everything that he did not experience himself. He famously wrote in the Discourse on Method; "I have a great aversion to ... accepting anything as true which is not known to me to be such." This commitment to skepticism and doubt was a departure from the philosophical and religious traditions that had preceded him but was a part of the broader Epistemological debate that manifested itself violently across the 17th century. Descartes wanted to return to the drawing board to first determine what can be known, a philosophic project that created the formal field of Metaphysics.

Skeptical doubt is the first principle of Descartes which arose from his own existential crises and doubts about the veracity of his own cognitive ability. His decision to forge a new path for Philosophy is rooted in the establishment of concept of *fundamentum inconcussum*, the "unshakeable foundation", first formulated in his work Meditationes de prima philosophia, or Meditations on First Philosophy:

> Since it's still me who doubts, I myself can no longer doubt this ego, even if it dreams or fantasizes. Thus rejecting everything that is even doubtful and accepting it as false, we can easily assume that there is no God, no heaven, no body; that we ourselves have neither hands nor feet, no body at all; but we cannot suppose that we who think such things are nothing; for it is a contradiction that what thinks does not exist at the time when it thinks. That is why the knowledge: "I think, therefore I am" (Latin: ego cogito, ergo sum) is the first and most certain of all, which emerges in orderly philosophizing.

From this foundation, Descartes then attempts to rebuild the cognitive faculty. At the crux of Descartes' philosophy is the idea that the mind and the body are separate and distinct entities. As he wrote in the "Meditations on First Philosophy," "I am not merely present in my body as a sailor is present in a ship, but I am very closely joined and, as it were, intermingled with it, so that I and the body form a unit." This idea, known as Cartesian dualism, has had a profound impact on Western philosophy and has been both celebrated and criticized over the centuries. "Cartesian Dualism" is a phrase anybody will know.

This system of doubt was not birthed out of negation, but out of piety. In "Meditations on First Philosophy" he writes "Whatever I perceive very clearly and distinctly is true." Doubt is not the result of Cartesian thinking, but certainty and freedom. It is an attempt to know apart from environmental factors, a movement towards a pure philosophy. To this idea, Descartes believed that only ideas that were clear and distinct could be considered true knowledge, creating an Epistemology upon which Empirical Science would be founded upon. Hegel notes this paradox of doubt proceeding knowledge:

> Descartes makes it the first requirement of philosophy that one must doubt everything, i.e. give up all presuppositions. De omnibus dubitandum est, was the first sentence of Cartesius, - this sinking of all presuppositions and determinations itself. However, it does not have the sense of skepticism, which does not set itself any other goal than doubting itself, that one should stop at this indecisiveness of the spirit, which has its freedom in it, but rather it has the sense that one must renounce all prejudice - i.e. all presuppositions, which are likewise immediately assumed to be true - and start from thinking, in order to come to something solid only from thinking, to gain a pure beginning. This is not the case with the skeptics; there doubt is the result.

> Descartes' doubting, not making a presupposition, because nothing is solid, certain, does not happen in the interest of freedom itself as such, that nothing is valid outside of freedom, nothing is in quality, way of a presupposition, of an external objective. Everything is unsolid insofar as I can abstract from it, i.e. think; pure thinking is abstraction from everything. The impulse of freedom lies at the bottom, but predominantly or in consciousness the purpose is to come to something solid, objective, - the

moment of the objective, not the moment of the subjective, that it is set, recognized, proven by me; but this interest falls into it, because from my thinking I want to come there. We do not have to consider the course of Descartes as consistently proven according to method; it is deep, inner progress, appearing naive. The spirit of his philosophy is knowledge, thought, unity of thinking and being.

Martin Heidegger, in his seminal work "Being and Time," saw Descartes' philosophy as a turning point in the history of Western thought, writing "Descartes transforms Being into an object, which the subject stands over against and represents." Heidegger believed that this transformation led to a problematic understanding of Being that characterized much of modern philosophy, but he admitted that Descartes' work also provided the basis for all subsequent anthropology. Descartes' philosophical revolution is sometimes said to have sparked modern anthropocentrism and subjectivism.

Heidegger muses on the metaphysics of Descartes in his 1955 *Was ist das die Philosoph*ie, where he states:

> For Descartes, however, what is true is measured in a different way. For him, the two of calculation, even the prosaic sobriety of planning are marks of a gestitudo. Not only this; even reason, which keeps itself free from all influence of the passions, is tuned as reason to confidence in the logical-mathematical insightfulness of its principles and rules. The specially adopted and unfolding corresponding to the assurance of the being of the existing is the philosophy. What this is - the philosophy, we get to know and know only if we learn how, in which way the philosophy is. It is in the way of the corresponding, which tunes itself to the voice of the being of the existing.

In his 1947 book Miracles, C.S. Lewis had a positive view of Descartes' philosophy, particularly his method of doubt and rationality, writing "Descartes, with his method of doubt, takes the foundations of his faith and life out of the shifting sands of experience and places them upon the rock of Reason." Pascal has a negative reading and regarded Descartes' views as a rationalist and mechanist, and accused him of deism:

> I cannot forgive Descartes; in all his philosophy, Descartes did his best to dispense with God. But Descartes could not avoid prodding God to set the world in motion with a snap of his lordly fingers; after that, he had no more use for God.

Hegel admired many parts of Descartes, but made a similar accusation to Pascal:

> Cartesian' determinations are of the kind that they suffice very well for mechanism, but not further; the representations of the other worldviews (e.g., vegetal and animal nature) are insufficient and therefore uninteresting.

Marx made this same observation that Descartes inadvertently created the foundation of Nominalism, which birthed his beloved Anti-Metaphysical Materialism:

"In his physics, Descartes had given matter self-creative power and conceived mechanical motion as its vital act. He had completely separated his physics from his metaphysics. Within his physics, matter is the only substance, the only ground of being and knowing. Mechanical French materialism joined the physics of Descartes in opposition to his metaphysics. His disciples were anti-metaphysicians by profession, namely physicists."

Kantian Reading

Immanuel Kant wrote extensively on Descartes' philosophy, having studied in his shadow, and in his "Critique of Pure Reason," he wrote, "Descartes was the first to bring to light the idea of a transcendental science, which is to contain a system of knowledge of the conditions of possibility of all knowledge." Descartes was the first to create a systematic metaphysical system. Compared to the complexity of the one Kant, creates, Descartes' metaphysics is child's play. The "I am" part of the Cogito Ergo Sum is problematic to Kant, since Being is not a predicate, and existence must be predicated in relation to another predicate, not a Subject. One of Kant's great tasks was to prove the existence of the Thing-in-Itself. He writes:

Descartes (although the latter was only a task, because of whose indissolubility, in Cartesian opinion, everyone was free to deny the existence of the physical world), the existence of the corporeal world, because it could never be answered satisfactorily), or with the mystical and enthusiastic one of Berkeley (against which and other similar fantasies our criticism rather contains the actual antidote).

…the empirical idealism of Descartes (although the latter was only a task, because of whose indissolubility, in Cartesian opinion, everyone was free to deny the existence of the physical world

The proof must therefore show that we also have experience of external things and not mere imagination. The demanded proof must therefore show that we also have experience of external things and not merely imagination; which cannot be done otherwise than by proving that even our inner experience, which Cartesius does not doubt, is only possible under the condition of external experience.

In his 1786 Metaphysical Foundations of Natural Science, he argues for the inevitable completeness of Newtonian Mechanics as a causal descriptor, but then in his 1764 Observations on the Sense of the Beautiful and the Sublime", he argues that beauty is outside of this Mechanistic Reductionism. Kant's Metaphysics exhibit this antinomy, and he attempts to establish the reality of the Soul and the material world through his Transcendental Idealism.

Hegelian reading

In his first Essay in the Journal of Critical Philosophy, Hegel describes broadly his approach to Philosophy and his views on the current state of philosophy in Europe. His view is dialectal: every new philosophy is the inevitable re-iteration of its historical predecessors. Philosophy proper is "a totality of knowledge produced by reflection" and "Transcendental philosophy is a science of the absolute". He is concerned with the future of philosophy and science because the Enlightenment thinkers wrongly conflated Science as knowledge itself, and partly blames Kant for continuing this Cartesian fallacy. This has created "An age that has such a multitude of philosophical systems in its history seems to created an indifference which life attains after it has tried itself in all forms".

Kant halted his logical analysis at the Soul (Seele), arguing that we cannot know the ordering of the internal workings of the Nous. This was part of a broader rejection of Cartesianism and Aristotelianism resulting in his rejection of traditional Catholic and Protestant Cosmo-Theology and developed an Onto-Theological conception of perception (something Kierkegaard, who generally detested the German Idealists, rifted upon). Hegel, wrestling with the interpretations and reception of Kant through Johann Gottlieb Fichte and Friedrich Schelling, rejected this truncated Epistemology and sought an absolute, scientific metaphysical system of knowing and rationalistic self-consciousness. Kant and Hegel share many philosophic roots, including the idea that the thinking "I" (Ich Denke) is the only possibility of a unified knowing. Even though they both criticize Cartesianism heavily, they still use a basic Cartesian conception of the Self. Knowledge is a function of Ontology, of Socratic self-awareness.

In his Lectures on the History of Philosophy, Hegel breaks out Philosophy into three broad Eras: The Greek era stemming from ancient Oriental Philosophy moving from Thales (600BC) to Plotinus (300 AD), The Scholastic period including Arab medieval thinkers, the Philosophy of the "New Age" starting from the Thirty Years' War with Bacon, Böhme and Descartes. Descartes Hegel identifies as the "true initiator of modern Philosophy" and we are still under his sway. In his early Jena writings, he identifies Cartesian Dualism as a broken Epistemology, a death, which all western rationalism was founded upon:

> Against Cartesian philosophy, which has expressed in philosophical form the generally spreading dualism in the culture of the more recent history of our north-western world - a dualism of which, as the demise of all old life, the quieter transformation of the public life of men as well as the louder political and religious revolutions in general are only differently colored outer sides - every side of living nature, as well as philosophy, had to seek means of rescue, just as against the general culture which it expresses; what has been done by philosophy in this respect, where it has been pure and open, has been treated with fury; where it has been done more concealed and confused, the mind has seized upon it all the more easily and remade it into the previous dualistic being. All the sciences have been founded on this death, and what was still scientific, that is, at least subjectively alive in them, time has killed completely, so that, if it were not directly the spirit of philosophy itself, which, submerged and constricted in this vast sea, feels the force of its growing wings all the stronger, even the boredom of the sciences - this edifice of an intellect abandoned by reason, which, worst of

all, with the borrowed name of either an enlightening or moral reason, has in the end also ruined theology - ought to make the whole flat expansion unbearable and at least excite a longing of wealth for a drop of fire, for a concentration of living contemplation and, after the dead has been known long enough, for a knowledge of the living which is possible through reason alone.

It is necessary to believe in the possibility of such real knowledge, not merely in that negative wandering or perennial shooting up of new forms, if a true effect is to be expected from a critique of them, namely, not a merely negative smashing of these limitations, but from it a paving of the way for the advent of true philosophy…

Even though Cartesius starts from "naïve empirical reasoning", to Hegel he still made critical correct assumptions, including that "Descartes proved freedom from the fact that the soul thinks, the will is unlimited; and this constitutes the perfection of man. This is quite correct."

Schopenhauer's Reading

Arthur Schopenhauer, in his "The World as Will and Representation" criticized Descartes' philosophy for its emphasis on reason and consciousness, which he believed ignored the underlying irrational nature of existence, writing "The subject, as pure knowing, is an illusion produced by the will." As Schopenhauer's self-described enemy Hegel notes "Descartes thus begins with the point of view of the I as the conscience par excellence". Likewise, Schopenhauer collapsed his Platonism to a divide between the Will and the World, negating the existence of the soul but upholding the basic platonic divide. In other words, Schopenhauer disagreed that there is an "I" or "Self", and that the Subject is only the irrational and unknowable Will. He writes:

> Cartesius is rightly considered the father of modern philosophy, first and in general, because he led reason to stand on its own two feet by teaching men to use their own heads, for which until then the Bible on the one hand and Aristotle on the other had functioned; but in particular and in a narrower sense, because he first brought to consciousness the problem around which all philosophizing since then has mainly revolved: the problem of the ideal and the real, i.e. the question of what is objective in our knowledge and what is subjective in it, i.e. what in it is to be attributed to things that are different from us and what is to be attributed to ourselves.

Nietzsche and the Nihilistic Collapse of the Self

Friedrich Nietzsche had a very critical view of Descartes' philosophy, despite utilizing his methods of doubt. He believed that the idea of a unified, rational self was a fiction, and wrote in "Beyond Good and Evil," "Descartes thought he had doubting in his power; but the doubt of the faith in his body and the senses led him to the very absurdity of the 'cogito.'"

Nietzsche's hatred of Descartes in indistinguishable from his hatred of

Socrates, because the root problem is that there is no "I" to know in the first place. Erasing the Platonism of Schopenhauer, Nietzsche argued there is no Self, no "Mind" and there is only material. Despite this, Nietzsche still used metacognitive concepts such as the Apollonian/ Dionysian archetypes which are metaphysical concepts, not rational. He credits Spinoza, just like Hegel, of finally collapsing the Mind-Body divide completely:

> Cartesius' philosophy has taken many unspeculative turns; he is immediately followed by Spinoza, who has penetrated to the whole consequence. He studied mainly the Cartesian philosophy, speaking in his terminology; the first writing of Spinoza are: *Principles of Cartesius*. The Spinozistic philosophy relates to the philosophy of Descartes only as a consistent execution, implementation of this principle. - To him, soul and body, thinking and being cease to be special things, each being a thing in itself. The dualism, which is present in the Cartesian system, Benedict Spinoza completely abolished, - as a Jew. This deep unity of his philosophy, as it was expressed in Europe, the spirit, infinite and finite identical in God, not as a third, is an echo of the Orient. The Oriental view of the absolute identity was directly brought closer to the European way of thinking and closer to the European, Cartesian philosophizing, was introduced into it.

Hegel makes a similar argument about Cartesian Epistemology inadvertently creating Spinoza's Materialism:

> Philosophy and exact science were not separated; only later did separation of the two occur...

> Only in Descartes this form is inappropriate; α) that there are two things, thought (soul) and body; β) God now appears as a third thing, outside of both, not the concept of unity and the two members not themselves concept. But it must not be forgotten that he says those first two are created substances. This belongs to the conception; created is not a definite thought. This reduction to the thought was then made by Spinoza.

Marxist Reading of Descartes

Karl Marx's reading of Descartes is indistinguishable from Ludwig Feuerbach. Feuerbach, in his "The Essence of Christianity," also criticized Descartes' emphasis on reason, which he saw as leading to a neglect of the embodied nature of human existence. He wrote, "The Cartesian ego is an abstraction, a mere product of thought, which has nothing in common with the real ego."

> By his well-known dubito, cogito, ergo sum, he wanted to emphasize the only certainty of subjective consciousness, in contrast to the problematic of everything else, and to express the great truth that the only thing that is really and necessarily given is self-consciousness. He said that the only thing that is really and necessarily given is self-consciousness, and that the only thing that is really and necessarily given is self-consciousness.

Feuerbach and Marx believed that Descartes and Locke were instrumental to French Materialism, and the basic elements of Cartesianism are still present:

> Just as Cartesian materialism leads into natural science proper, so the other direction of French materialism leads directly into socialism and communism… Cartesian materialism exists to this day in France. It has its great successes in mechanical natural science, which, to speak accurately and in the prosaic sense, will be least reproached for romanticism.

> We do not have to go into detail about French materialism, which derives directly from Descartes, any more than we have to go into detail about the French school of Newton and the development of French natural science in general.

In other works, Pierre Bayle (one of Marx's great heroes) finally defeated the Dualistic Metaphysics in Descartes, and kept the rationalism which Spinoza and Leibniz failed to remove. This understanding comes exclusively from Ludwig Feuerbach's reading and interpretation of Bayle, whom he wrote on extensively.

The Cartesian Foundation of Modern Psychology

Sigmund Freud, in his work on psychoanalysis, also had a critical view of Descartes' philosophy from a similar perspective of Schopenhauer. Much of Freud's emphasis on the reality of the internal life of the psyche was borrowed from Schopenhauer, which he tried to reconcile with Feuerbach's materialism. He believed that Descartes' emphasis on reason and consciousness ignored the role of the unconscious mind in human behavior. In "The Ego and the Id" he wrote "It is Descartes' error to locate the ego where consciousness is, and to attribute to it the whole of psychic life." Descartes argued that dreams can also be real, or true, since they exist within a mathematical world. Freud's entire theory of dreams is based on this correlation between a scientific, mathematical world and the reality of the mind.

Carl Jung, in his work on psychology and mythology, saw Descartes' philosophy as a significant influence on the development of the Western ego. However, he also believed that this emphasis on reason and rationality had led to a neglect of the irrational and unconscious aspects of human experience. In "The Archetypes and the Collective Unconscious," he wrote, "The Cartesian cogito is a rationalistic, one-sided view that neglects the reality of the unconscious psyche."

Carl Jung's argument is quite similar to Søren Kierkegaard's, displaying how deeply Socratic Jungian Philosophy is. Kierkegaard, in his "Concluding Unscientific Postscript," criticized Descartes' philosophy for its emphasis on reason and its neglect of subjective experience. He wrote, "In Descartes' philosophy, the single individual does not exist; rather, there is only the universal, the general, the abstract." Kierkegaard believed that this neglect of individual experience was a fundamental flaw in Descartes' philosophy. On a broad Epistemological level, Kierkegaard refuted Descartes' idea that there is a "foundation" of knowledge that can be universally known- rather, there are always going to be unprovable a priori assumptions.

Cartesius' dualistic philosophy of the mind is the foundation of all modern Psychology. This Dualism helped pave the way for the development of modern psychology, and is paltry in both Freud and Jung. In Freud, Feuerbach's Materialism is clashing with Cartesius' Mind-body Dualism. There must be an "I", both individual and collective, for Psychology to have any utility. In the therapeutic telos, pure Newtonian mechanics reducing all reality to physio-chemical reactions is always irrelevant and the internal realities of Noumena must be considered more "real" than the material world. Even the dedicated Atheist and Feuerbachian Materialist Freud had to view Psychological experiences as real, or meta-real; a Gestalt reality which is more than the sum of its material parts.

The East and Cartesius the Man

It is no surprise that the Reformation's Iconoclasm and the desecration of the Eucharist through Zwinglian Memorialism, now practiced by virtually all "bible-believing" Christians coincided with this disenchantment of reality, and the building of a wall between the mind and body, the material and the immaterial. Descartes was capturing the Zeitgest of his time, for the wall between Geist and the Material had already be built by the Nominalism of Luther's Claritas Scriptura, which asserted that the mind can observe and interpret without a priori assumptions.

As a Catholic living in Protestant Countries (Calvinist France and Netherlands, Evangelical Sweden) and living through the violence of the 30 years wars, it is no wonder that Descartes sought a common method for discerning truth. Some have accused him of shifting the root or foundation of truth from God to Human perception, but this is still today deeply argued- Hegel believed he set up this possibility but did not make the move himself.. Protestantism had already shifted the loci of truth from a relational predicate to subjective interpretation.

Christos Yannaras writes of the Psychological effect of Nominalism via Descartes:

> The Cartesian understanding of the person has affected the whole of Western thought, including Christian theology. It has led to a view of the human person as an isolated and autonomous individual, rather than as a relational and embodied being. This has had a negative impact on our understanding of the nature of God, the Church, and the world, and has led to a spiritual and moral crisis in the West.

Descartes never intended to do this, but this was the impact of Descartes' Dualism, even though he rejected this absolute divide himself: ""I am not merely present in my body as a sailor is present in a ship, but I am very closely joined and, as it were, intermingled with it, so that I and the body form a unit." Descartes himself was deeply concerned with the possibility that his perception is flawed. In he Meditations on the Foundations of Philosophy, he writes of a possible malevolent force capable of duping his perception:

> Well, if he deceives me, there is no doubt that I am. He deceives me as much as he can, but he will never bring it about that I am nothing as long as I think I am something. And so, after pondering everything more than enough, I finally come to the conclusion that this sentence: "I am, I exist" (Latin ego

sum, ego existo), whenever I say it or in think, is necessarily true.

This Socratic self-doubt is nothing new in Theology. Augustine already posited this Mind-Body distinction problem in the 5th century in his De civitate Dei contra Paganos, The City of God:

> If I am mistaken, I am. For he who is not, of course, cannot be deceived. And by this I am, if I am mistaken. Since then I am, if I am mistaken, how am I mistaken to be, when is it certain that I am if I am mistaken?

Descartes never encountered Orthodoxy significantly- his foray into Greek history was brief, and in his travels never made it far enough East. But this deep and radical doubting is inherent to the violent warfare with the flesh found in Easter Ascetics. But in Eastern Mysticism, the question whether the "guarantee" of truth is an external agent or internal certainty is irrelevant. In the last 2,000 years, Atheism has never can found a foothold in the East, but in the West it finds its origin and has flourished. How much Descartes had to do with this is a complex question- in many ways, he was the product of his time.

Marx made the observation that the 17th century introduced Nominalism, resulting from the rationalization of Christianity into logical theorems, as the foundation of Atheism, an accusation Eastern Orthodoxy has been making of Western Theology since the Great Schism:

> To accomplish this miracle, he resorted to God's omnipotence, i.e. he forced theology itself to preach materialism. He was a nominalist above all. Nominalism is found as a main element among the English materialists, as it is the first expression of materialism in general.

In this view, Descartes was simply caught up in broader forces of history. Certainly, Orthodoxy maintains the existence of a consciousness- material distinction, but through Theantropic Theology, still richly alive in the East but flattened and rationalized in the West, demands that the material is not metaphysically divided from the Mind. As God became Material Man, so the Cartesian Distinction is irrelevant at best. The gulf has a bridge built across it. And this union is restored, renewed and constellated into the material mind weekly; the Eucharist unites the natural and the supernatural continuously, the divine liturgy breaking the bond between worlds, the apotheosis and intersection of all realities. The Incarnation, manifest in holy ritual, binds reality unto itself. We, as body-soul dualities we participate in the Logos through the experience of consciousness.

Thus, the fulfillment of the Socratic, Delphic command to "know thyself", the basis of any real, existentialist knowledge, is only found through Theosis- the constellation of the Archetype of Consciousness (Hegel) or the Archetype of Self-Consciousness (Jung). From the Eastern Orthodox view, Cartesianism is incomplete, for this absolute knowledge of the self is only realized by relational, embodied Theosis through the imitation and participation in the Archetype of Self-Consciousness, returning full circle to the Psalmist- "The fear of the Lord is the beginning of all knowledge".

Tim Newcomb
Stuttgart, Germany
Spring 2023

Timeline of Descartes Life & Works

1596
René Descartes is born in La Haye en Touraine, France.

1616
Descartes graduates from the University of Poitiers with a law degree.

1618-1648
Thirty Years' War ravages Europe.

1620
Descartes begins his military service in the Dutch army.

1628
Descartes begins to write his first major work, "Rules for the Direction of the Mind."

1633
Galileo is put on trial for heresy, leading Descartes to refrain from publishing his own scientific findings.

1637
Descartes publishes "Discourse on the Method," which outlines his philosophy and method of systematic doubt.

1641
Descartes publishes "Meditations on First Philosophy," in which he introduces his famous phrase, "I think, therefore I am."

1642
English mathematician and physicist Isaac Newton is born, and Galileo Galilei dies

1644
Descartes meets Queen Christina of Sweden and begins a correspondence with her.

1648
Peace of Westphalia ends Thirty Years' War and establishes the modern system of sovereign nation-states.

1649
Descartes dies in Stockholm, Sweden.

1687
Isaac Newton publishes "Philosophiæ Naturalis Principia Mathematica," which provides a mathematical foundation for physics that would come to supersede Descartes' ideas.

Glossary of Cartesian Terminology

Cogito, ergo sum

His most famous moniker. Latin for "I think, therefore I am," a famous phrase coined by Descartes in his "Meditations on First Philosophy." He writes, "I am, I exist, is necessarily true every time I conceive of it in my mind."

Dualism

The belief that there are two distinct substances in the world, mind and body, that exist separately. Descartes famously held this view and wrote, "There is a great difference between mind and body, inasmuch as body is by nature always divisible, and the mind is entirely indivisible."

Methodological skepticism

A method of doubt used by Descartes to systematically doubt everything he believed to be true in order to arrive at indubitable knowledge. He writes, "I resolved to assume that everything which I formerly accepted as the most true was false."

Innate ideas

The idea that some ideas are born within us, rather than being learned through experience. Descartes believed in the existence of innate ideas and wrote, "There is nothing which is easier for me than to know the nature of God...this idea of God, or of a supremely perfect being, is innate in me."

Clear and distinct ideas

Ideas that are so clear and distinct that they cannot be doubted. Descartes believed that these were the only ideas that could be relied upon as true. He writes, "Whatever I perceive very clearly and distinctly is true."

Substance

A fundamental entity that exists independently and is capable of existing on its own. Descartes believed that both mind and body were separate substances. He writes, "By substance, I understand that which exists in such a way as to depend on no other thing for its existence."

Objective reality

The reality of a thing as it exists outside of the mind. Descartes believed that objective reality was the only true reality. He writes, "I conclude that the only reality of things is the objective reality of the ideas."

Ontological argument

A type of argument that attempts to prove the existence of God based on the concept of God as a supremely perfect being. Descartes formulated an ontological argument in his "Meditations on First Philosophy." He writes, "The idea of God, by which I understand a supremely perfect being, exists in me as a true and immutable nature."

Dualism
Dualism is a philosophical view that postulates the existence of two distinct substances. Descartes coined the term dualism to explain the distinction between the material world (res extensa) and the spiritual world (res cogitans).

Method
Method refers to a systematic approach to the study of natural phenomena. Descartes advocated a methodical approach to acquiring knowledge and attaining truth.

Rationalism
Rationalism is a philosophy that states that knowledge and truth can be achieved through reason and logical thinking. Descartes is considered the father of rationalism and believed that reason is the best way to find truth, although this reason must be based in certainty of the self.

Doubt (Zweifel)
Doubt is a state of uncertainty or indecision that relates to knowledge and truth. Descartes advocated the systematic use of doubt to find truth and rule out false beliefs.

Intuition
Intuition refers to the ability to understand or know without conscious thought. Descartes believed in the power of intuition as a method of knowing truth.

Inner perception (Innere Wahrnehmung)
Inner perception refers to the awareness of mental states such as beliefs, thoughts and emotions. Descartes saw inner perception as evidence for the existence of consciousness and mind.

Substance (Substanz)
Substance refers to an independent and unchanging object that exists by itself. Descartes distinguished between material substance and mental substance.

Causality (Kausalität)
Causality refers to the relationship between cause and effect. Descartes saw causality as a fundamental concept in natural philosophy.

Deduction (Deduktion)
Deduction refers to the logical deduction of a conclusion from a set of premises. Descartes believed that deduction is a necessary tool for the attainment of truth.

Meditation
Meditation refers to contemplative reflection on philosophical topics. Descartes' writings "Meditations on First Philosophy" refer to his method of meditation to achieve truth.

Proof of God (Gottesbeweis)
Descartes developed an ontological proof for the existence of God, which states that the idea of God exists in our minds independently of our experience and must therefore be real.

Descartes' Major Works

1619 Abstract of Music

René Descartes is one of the most influential philosophers in the history of Western thought. He wrote extensively on topics ranging from mathematics to metaphysics and left many unpublished manuscripts. His 1619 Abstract of Music, is a treatise on the mathematical principles of music. Descartes composed this treatise in 1618, during his stay in Breda, when he was only 22 years old. It was not printed until after his death: Compendium musicæ. Descartes believed that music could be explained in terms of the laws of mathematics and that the emotions that music evokes could be understood in terms of the way in which it affects the body, something which was a novel idea at the time.

This idea has been echoed by other philosophers such as Gottfried Leibniz, who wrote, "Music is the pleasure the human mind experiences from counting without being aware that it is counting." Similarly, Immanuel Kant expanded upon this in his lengthy lectures on Aesthetics -"Music is the only art which can calm the agitations of the soul; it is one of the most magnificent and delightful presents God has given us." These philosophers recognized the unique ability of music to affect the human mind and emotions, and Descartes' mathematical approach to understanding music was an important contribution to the field.

1622 Treatise on Man

Here he argues that the human body can be understood as a machine. This mechanistic view of the body was influential in the development of modern science and has been further developed by other philosophers such as Julien Offray de La Mettrie, who wrote, "Man is nothing but a machine, a wonderfully complex machine." Similarly, Thomas Hobbes wrote, "Nature hath made men so equal in the faculties of body and mind as that, though there be found one man sometimes manifestly stronger in body or of quicker mind than another, yet when all is reckoned together the difference between man and man is not so considerable as that one man can thereupon claim to himself any benefit to which another may not pretend as well as he." These philosophers recognized the importance of understanding the body and mind in mechanistic terms, and Descartes' Treatise on Man was an important contribution to this way of thinking.

1637 Discourse on Method

In Descartes' 1637 Discourse on Method, he outlines his method for arriving at certain knowledge. He is attempting to establish a knowledge that is certain and indubitable. He emphasizes the importance of doubting everything that can be doubted and then proceeding from the things that are certain to those that are less certain. Descartes also discusses the role of mathematics in the sciences and argues that mathematics provides a sure foundation for knowledge. This method has been influential in the development of modern science and has been praised by other philosophers such as John Locke, who wrote, "Our business here is not to know all things, but those which concern our conduct. If we can find out those measures whereby a rational creature, put in that state in which man is in this world, may and ought to govern his opinions and actions depending thereon, we need not be troubled that some other things escape our knowledge." Similarly, David Hume wrote, "The wise man proportions his belief to the evidence." These philosophers recognized the importance of using reason and evidence to arrive at certain knowledge, and Descartes' Discourse on Method was an important contribution to this way of thinking.

1637 Treatise on Mechanics

Here Descartes applies his mathematical approach to understanding the physical world. This work has been influential in the development of modern physics and has been praised by other philosophers such as Isaac Newton, who wrote, "I know not what I may appear to the world, but to myself I seem to have been only like a boy playing on the seashore, and diverting myself in now and then finding a smoother pebble or a prettier shell than ordinary, whilst the great ocean of truth lay all undiscovered before me." Similarly, Albert Einstein wrote, "Pure mathematics is in its way, the poetry of logical ideas." These philosophers recognized the importance of mathematics in understanding the physical world, and Descartes' Treatise on Mechanics was an important contribution to this way of thinking.

1641 Meditations on First Philosophy

In his 1641 Meditations on First Philosophy, Descartes famously proclaimed, "Cogito, ergo sum" ("I think, therefore I am"). This statement has become one of the most famous and widely quoted in the history of philosophy. Descartes used this statement as a starting point for his argument that the only thing that can be known with certainty is that one exists as a thinking thing. He went on to argue that knowledge of the external world can only be attained through the use of reason, and that sensory experience is not a reliable guide to truth.

This work has been influential in the development of modern philosophy and has been praised by other philosophers such as Immanuel Kant, who wrote, "All our knowledge begins with the senses, proceeds then to the understanding, and ends with reason. There is nothing higher than reason." Similarly, René Guénon wrote, "The only real philosophy is that which enables us to grasp the ultimate reality; it is the only one which can really satisfy man's aspirations." These philosophers recognized the importance of understanding the ultimate reality and the limits of human knowledge, and Descartes' Meditations on First Philosophy was an important contribution to this way of thinking.

1644 Principles of Philosophy (Principia philosophiae)

In Descartes' 1644 Principles of Philosophy, he presents a comprehensive overview of his philosophy. This work has been influential in the development of modern philosophy and has been praised by other philosophers such as Baruch Spinoza, who wrote, "All things excellent are as difficult as they are rare." Similarly, Friedrich Nietzsche wrote, "The essence of all beautiful art, all great art, is gratitude." These philosophers recognized the difficulty of achieving excellence in philosophy and the importance of expressing gratitude for those who have contributed to the field, and Descartes' Principles of Philosophy was an important contribution to this way of thinking.

1649 The Passions of the Soul

In Descartes' 1649 The Passions of the Soul, he examines the emotions and their impact on human behavior. This work has been influential in the development of modern psychology and has been praised by other philosophers such as Jean-Jacques

Rousseau, who wrote, "Man is born free, and everywhere he is in chains." Similarly, Sigmund Freud wrote, "The voice of the intellect is a soft one, but it does not rest until it has gained a hearing." These philosophers recognized the importance of understanding human behavior and the impact of emotions, and Descartes' The Passions of the Soul was an important contribution to this way of thinking.

1664 The World, or Treatise of the Light

Descartes' theory of light and vision revolutionized the way we understand these phenomena. He argued that light is composed of minute particles that travel in straight lines, and that vision is the result of the intersection of these particles with the eye. This theory has been influential in the development of modern optics and has had a significant impact on our understanding of the physical world.

This work has been influential in the development of modern physics and has been praised by other philosophers such as Gottfried Leibniz, who wrote, "Nothing takes place in the world whose meaning is not that of some maximum or minimum." Similarly, James Clerk Maxwell wrote, "The truth of a theory is in your mind, not in your eyes." These philosophers recognized the importance of understanding the physical world and the role of theory in doing so, and

Printed in Great Britain
by Amazon